THE
GENERATIONAL
ADVANTAGE

THE GENERATIONAL ADVANTAGE

HOW TO **LEAD, COMMUNICATE,**
AND **DRIVE PERFORMANCE**
ACROSS GENERATIONS

KAMBER PARKER BOWDEN

PALMETTO
PUBLISHING
Charleston, SC
www.PalmettoPublishing.com

Copyright © 2025 by Kamber Parker Bowden

All rights reserved.

No portion of this book may be reproduced, stored in a retrieval system, or transmitted in any form by any means–electronic, mechanical, photocopy, recording, or other–except for brief quotations in printed reviews, without prior permission of the author.

Hardcover ISBN: 9798318810985
Paperback ISBN: 9798822975163
eBook ISBN: 9798822975170

"Seek first to understand, then to be understood."
—**Stephen R. Covey**

I dedicate this book to the original young professional interviewees, who generously shared their time and stories. Your openness was the origin story of my business —and for that, I am forever grateful.

CONTENTS

Preface xiii

Chapter 1: The Generational Advantage 1

Chapter 2: The Challenges: *Generational Gaps in Today's Workforce* 11

Chapter 3: The Talent Impact Process: *A New Era of Workforce Strategy* 23

Chapter 4: Generational Excellence: *Building Bridges* 31

Chapter 5: Attracting Talent: *Creating a Magnetic Brand* 41

Chapter 6: Onboarding and Development Reimagined 51

Chapter 7: Retention and Activation: *Turning Talent into Loyalty* 63

Chapter 8: Communication and Expectations: *Creating Connection* 75

Chapter 9: Culture: *The Foundation for Multigenerational Success* 87

Chapter 10: Data-Driven Decisions: *The Generational Playbook* 97

Chapter 11: The Formula: *Putting the Pieces Together* 107

Chapter 12: The Future of Work: *Thriving in the AI-Driven, Multigenerational Era* 115

Acknowledgements 121

Sources 123

Generational change is inevitable. Preparation is a choice.
—**Kamber Parker Bowden**

PREFACE

The cost of miscommunication across generations? Millions of dollars, every day.

I didn't realize this when I was twenty-one, sitting in my first so-called "dream job," confused and frustrated by a workplace that didn't match what I'd been promised. I thought I was the problem.

But after thousands of interviews with professionals across every generation, I've learned that the real issue isn't individual—it's generational.

This book is the culmination of nearly five thousand interviews—and counting—with young professionals (YoPros) across the country, paired with insights from conversations with over ten thousand professionals across generations during keynotes, workshops, programs, and workforce planning. What started as a deep dive into the unique challenges and opportunities faced by the youngest members of the workforce quickly evolved into something broader—and more powerful.

In my earliest conversations, I realized the disconnects between young professionals and their employers weren't isolated incidents. Leaders from every generation shared frustrations about retaining and developing their teams while young employees expressed confusion, dissatisfaction, and burnout. As I expanded my work, it became clear that the solution to these challenges wasn't about focusing on one generation—it was about developing understanding and collaboration between all generations in the workforce. This isn't about catering to younger workers or making things easier for anyone—it's about ensuring your workforce operates at peak efficiency.

The reality is that high turnover, miscommunication, and disengagement cost companies time, money, and productivity. Understanding generational dynamics isn't about changing everything to suit one group; it's about identifying ways to improve performance across the board.

That's what this book is about.

When you understand how each generation shows up, leads, and works, you gain an advantage. *A Generational Advantage.*

But let me take you back to the beginning because my personal story is at the heart of why Generational Performance Solutions (GPS), formerly YoPro Know, exists.

At twenty-one, I had landed the so-called perfect job. Fresh out of college, I dove headfirst into the insurance industry, eager to build a career and make my mark. But within a year, I was disillusioned. What had seemed so perfect on paper felt misaligned in practice, leaving me confused, frustrated, and unsure of my next steps.

I started asking my peers about their experiences, curious if my struggles were unique or part of a larger pattern. What I discovered was staggering: I wasn't alone. Many of my friends—and their friends—were navigating similar challenges, leaving one job after another by the age of twenty-three. The common thread? A fundamental disconnect between what these young professionals expected and what their workplaces delivered. I knew then that someone needed to address this gap. And if no one else would, I decided to take it on.

That bold decision guided much of my twenties—and my entire career!

What began as a side project, a space to share interviews and insights, quickly gained traction. I realized there was a hunger for real, actionable solutions to workforce challenges, particularly those rooted in generational differences. Encouraged by a few wise mentors who told me I was onto something, I took a leap and began transforming my passion project into a consulting firm using data and storytelling to help organizations reimagine how they attract, engage, and retain talent.

PREFACE

Think about the day-to-day challenges you experience in your workplace. These were the nuisances that leaders wanted answers to, and we were piecing together solutions by talking to young talent! From communication and flexibility to technology and culture, I set out with the goal of helping organizations solve their most critical challenges that kept them up at night. Once organizations recognized I had solutions with data to back them up and a few gracious leaders opened their doors for me, the work started to come.

The wise mentors noted above played a pivotal role in shaping the direction of YoPro Know and what is now Generational Performance Solutions. Their encouragement helped me see the potential in my work, but I've come to learn that mentorship is not solely a one-way street. Without a bit of persistent (but pleasant, so I've been told!) nudging, I might never have earned their time or support. These leaders—from my early career in Chattanooga, Tennessee, to my current home in Greenville, South Carolina—pushed me to see what I couldn't yet envision. The interviews, stories, and data I'd collected weren't just interesting. They were the foundation for solutions that companies needed.

As an early twentysomething, it was hard to fathom how I might accomplish what my mentors advised me to do, but I soon realized just how right they were. The interviews, stories, and data I had collected from the start would help this company lay down its roots as a revenue-generating business. It became clear to me shortly after that, but the question became *how do I do it?*

I know we're just a few pages in and you might not know me yet, but let me just share something with you. This was a scary thing to do as a young professional! I was on my second job at this point, working in fundraising at a small local nonprofit in South Carolina, and realized I had a choice. I could either A) take the advice of my mentors and make this into more than just a passion project, and really help organizations or B) keep interviewing people and let this thing roll on for however long it could go.

While you know which route I ended up taking, for what it's worth, it was *not* the easy choice. I say that I was a team of one for many years until I hired my first employee; however, the truth is I had a lot of help along the way.

Fast forward to today, and GPS is no longer a one-person operation. In 2022, I had the privilege of assembling an exceptional, multigenerational team that has elevated our work to new heights. Together, we've expanded our reach, partnering with organizations across the nation—and more recently, internationally—to address workforce challenges. Our mission is to help organizations save time, enhance performance, and drive purpose-driven profitability. Rooted in data, we use our research to demystify generational differences through training and keynotes, workforce advising, and strategic implementation.

Since we've built a team of our own, we've experienced some of the very challenges that we help our clients work through, including hiring the right (and wrong) talent, onboarding, developing and retaining talent, and communicating with that talent. These experiences have helped us practice what we preach, so not only do I have the tales of clients to share with you throughout this book, but I have our own experiences as a team as well. I've felt the frustrations you have felt and understand the challenges that come from growing, leading, and managing a multigenerational workforce. We also know the successes that come when our team's performance is maximized, and I will share that with you too.

This book reflects the "what got us here" part of GPS's journey. It captures lessons learned, insights gained, and proven strategies that leaders can use to transform their multigenerational workforces. If you're tired of investing precious time, resources, and training into team members only to see them walk out the door within a year, this book is for you.

PREFACE

Why Should You Read This Book?

Whether you're a leader struggling to connect with younger employees, an HR professional looking to bridge generational divides, or someone who's simply curious about how workplaces can evolve for the better, this book is for you.

This book is for leaders and any professionals looking to explore ways to make our workforce stronger.

In the pages ahead, you'll learn how to:

1. Communicate effectively with the next generation of talent to build trust and connection.
2. Enhance your multigenerational workforce so that all generations thrive and perform at the highest level.
3. Leverage proven solutions to position your company for long-term success.

This isn't just another business book. It's a practical, actionable guide designed to give you what I call the Generational Advantage, or the notion of leveraging the unique strengths, skills, and perspectives of different generations in the workplace to ignite collaboration and communication, drive profitability, and enhance overall productivity. By embracing and integrating these unique contributions, organizations can gain a competitive edge and optimize team performance while achieving their goals.

I have spent the last several years reading dozens of books about generations, and while each generation has its own unique attributes, I'm not here to bring you another book about Gen Z and Gen Y (millennials). I'm here to bring you a new kind of generation book, one that will help you start seeing results and one that is less about differences between generations—and more about the synergies instead. Together, we'll focus on the use of real-world case studies with our national clients and share how you can leverage our data to motivate your own workforce and see results.

Why This Book Now?

Today's workplace is undergoing a seismic shift. As we navigate this post-pandemic workplace, four generations are working side by side: baby boomers and Gen X in senior roles, millennials beginning to sit in leadership positions, and Gen Z entering their first and second jobs with Gen Alpha close behind. This already complex landscape is further compounded by the rise of hybrid work models, return-to-office mandates, rapid advancements in AI, and shifting workforce values. Organizations are navigating uncharted territory, and the challenges are only becoming more pronounced.

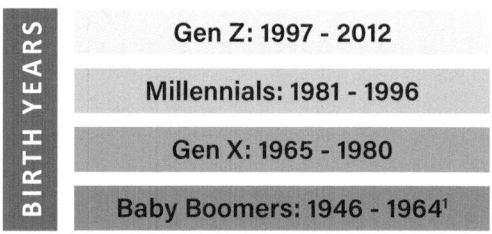

Let me share three critical realities shaping the future of work with you.

The first, and to no one's surprise, is that we are witnessing an aging workforce exit. The Great Resignation that followed the pandemic saw baby boomers leaving the workforce at unprecedented rates, creating a widening leadership gap.

Second, the US is facing a declining birth rate,[2] which means fewer future young professionals to fill the roles left behind by retiring generations. And third, we are witnessing a surge in entrepreneurship and innovation among Gen Z.[3] Many members of this generation are bypassing traditional corporate roles to forge their own paths, leaving industries struggling to tap into their potential. Without action, companies risk being left behind.

What happens if we don't adapt as a workforce? Communication breakdowns will lead to frustration. Retention rates will plummet as top talent seeks more fulfilling—and flexible—opportunities elsewhere. Institutional knowledge will be lost as experienced employees retire without passing it on to younger generations. These challenges are not hypothetical—they are the inevitable outcomes of inaction. Adapting to these changes isn't about making work "easier" for employees—it's about making business run better. I have seen companies that get ahead of these generational shifts see stronger performance, lower turnover costs, and more effective teams. Leaders who ignore these realities will find themselves losing talent and profitability to those who don't.

But here's the good news: The stakes may be high, but the opportunity is even greater. By understanding generational dynamics and implementing intentional processes, organizations can cultivate higher performance, stronger engagement, and a thriving culture that attracts and retains talent for years to come.

I would be remiss not to mention the obvious: The workplace will *always* change. New generations will rise, technology will advance, and leadership strategies will evolve. While some specifics in this book may shift over time, such as new generations and technology, the principles of adaptability, collaboration, and generational awareness will remain the foundation of strong leadership.

The future of your workforce doesn't have to be a guessing game. It's time to take control, embrace the challenges ahead, and create workplaces where talent from all generations collaborates toward a shared vision of success.

This is *the Generational Advantage*: not a trend, not a theory, but a competitive edge. You don't have to like change, but you do have to outlast those who resist it. So, what's your next move?

CHAPTER 1

THE GENERATIONAL ADVANTAGE

According to Gallup, 42 percent of employee turnover is preventable but often ignored.[4] Leaders who fail to recognize the generational shifts in the workplace are doing more than losing employees—they're losing their competitive edge.

If you don't understand and adapt to generational shifts in the workplace, your company will lose top talent, fall behind competitors, and struggle to grow. But if you get it right, you'll have the most productive, profitable, and engaged workforce of your career. In this book, I will show you how to make that happen.

When we talk about generations in the workplace, it's personal. You, me, everyone reading this—we all belong to one. Some of us might even straddle the line between two generations, or what we call "cuspers." And yet when we hear generational stereotypes—"Gen Z is lazy," "Millennials just want praise," "Boomers hate technology"—we laugh, nod, or bristle. These stereotypes may be exaggerated, but they highlight a deeper truth: *Misunderstanding generations hurts us all.* This applies both inside and outside of your office. In fact, I always mention to my audiences that they can take this information and apply it to their children, parents, and even grandparents. What I'm trying to say is that your life is a canvas for multigenerational research!

Stereotyping forges conflict where there could be collaboration. It builds resentment where there could be respect. And most importantly, it keeps companies from reaching their full potential and seeing the results they want.

As we explore generational insights in this book, it's important to remember that we're working with patterns—not prescriptions. When we reference Gen Z or Baby Boomers, we're talking about generational averages—general trends backed by data—not rigid rules. Every generation includes individuals who break the mold. Maybe your most tech-savvy team member is a Boomer who prefers texting and loves AI. Or maybe your Gen Z employee thrives on in-person meetings and formal communication. These outliers aren't exceptions to dismiss—they're reminders that assuming anything based solely on age is a recipe for miscommunication and missed opportunities. Generational data gives us a lens, not a label. The goal isn't to box people in—but to open up better ways of leading, connecting, and understanding each other.

This book offers a new way forward by walking you through our proprietary process, the Talent Impact Process. Our seven-part model outlines strategies to enhance your organization's generational dynamics and promote maximized performance through cross-generational talent integration. Instead of focusing on what divides us, we'll explore strategies, tools, and real-life stories to help leaders build thriving, multigenerational workforces where everyone, regardless of age or background, contributes and feels valued. Businesses that understand how to effectively manage multigenerational teams gain a competitive advantage by improving retention, increasing collaboration, and driving profitability. A well-run team, regardless of age, is a productive and profitable one.

KEYNOTE COMPANION

> Let's keep the momentum going. If you heard my keynote or attended a workshop, this book is your step-by-step guide to applying what you learned.

This is not only a book about how to understand young talent and the next generation. It's about building organizations where all generations thrive together. When you utilize the outlined process in this book, you will see the Generational Advantage take shape in your organization.

> Dive deeper with your downloadable worksheet and apply what you've learned right away. Visit:
> https://thegenerationaladvantage.com/get-downloads/

To fully understand the opportunities within today's multigenerational workforce, we must first explore the shifting dynamics and priorities shaping the workplace landscape.

The Reality of Work Today

1. The Demand for Flexibility
Across generations, workplace flexibility has emerged as a critical priority, specifically in the post-pandemic workplace we find ourselves in today.

According to a Generational Performance Solutions' 2024 workforce survey, 68 percent of young professionals tell us they now prefer a hybrid model blending in-office and remote work. Over 80 percent of young professionals report holding at least five jobs by the age of thirty, showcasing a shift toward entrepreneurship and innovation, which is likely due to the thousands of influencers their age who have made their business mark on their own.

But here's the question every leader needs to ask: What workplace model (i.e., 100 percent in-office, hybrid, or 100 percent remote) will help drive our team's performance, profitability, and purpose?

While I can't answer that question for you, I can recommend that you take a hard look at your current workplace model. Start by asking yourself:

- Do you need everyone in the office 100 percent of the time?
- Can your team function remotely 100 percent of the time?
- Or, does a hybrid model make the most sense for you?

Here's a tip: "Hybrid" doesn't mean the same thing to everyone. To some, it's a few days in the office each week; to others, it's full autonomy over where and how they work. At its core, though, hybrid really comes down to flexibility. And let's be honest for a second—I haven't met anyone from any generation who doesn't want some version of that!

Whatever flexibility looks like for your organization, the key is to communicate it clearly, implement it thoughtfully, and refine it as you go. Your team will thank you for it—and your results will too.

Case Study: How a National Law Firm Improved Retention with Strategic Flexibility
Take this national law firm we worked with a few years ago as an example. They were losing high-performing employees to competitors offering remote options. Recognizing the trend, leadership implemented a hybrid policy that not only allowed employees to work remotely two days a week but also introduced "flex Fridays" for team well-being. Within a year, turnover dropped by 22 percent, and employee satisfaction scores skyrocketed.

Despite what you might be thinking, this is not another trend; it's a shift. Employees across all age groups—parents of young children, mid-career professionals, and entry-level talent—seek control over their schedules. Leaders who embrace flexibility will not only retain talent for years to come but also boost team confidence and productivity.

2. Beyond the Paycheck

Compensation matters—but it's not enough. Employees across generations want to feel that their work aligns with their values and contributes to something meaningful. You don't have to be a "purpose-driven" company to understand this reality: Employees who feel a sense of ownership and alignment with their work perform better. If employees believe in what they do, they work harder and stay longer—meaning better retention, lower hiring costs, and a stronger business. Almost weekly I have conversations with young professionals who share how much their organization's mission means to them—and what it means when it does not mean as much!

A Generational Performance Solutions' 2023 workforce survey highlighted 60 percent of employees who cited purpose and culture as top factors in choosing an employer. Companies with strong missions and visions—like social impact or innovation—outperform their peers in attracting and retaining talent time and time again.

> **Case Study: Patagonia's Purpose-Driven Success**
> Patagonia, known for its environmental activism, exemplifies how culture can drive performance. Employees across generations feel connected to the company's mission of sustainability, and flexible benefits like paid volunteer hours reflect these values. This alignment of purpose and action has made Patagonia a talent magnet with one of the lowest turnover rates in its industry.[5]
>
> We'll come back to this conversation of "Beyond the Paycheck" later in this book.

3. Communication Crossroads

Generational communication styles differ, but they don't have to clash. While the Gen Z majority may prefer internal messaging channels like Slack or text messaging, boomers often favor email or in-person meetings. Without clear expectations, these differences can lead to miscommunication and frustration.

Take this example for context. At a midsize marketing agency, a Gen X team leader sent detailed emails expecting thoughtful responses within a day or two. Meanwhile, a millennial employee, who might prefer internal messaging such as Slack or Teams, grew frustrated by the lack of quick feedback. After adopting clearer communication guidelines—including when to email versus use Slack—the team saw a noticeable improvement in efficiency and team connection.

Good communication is truly not about catering to one group, but rather, it's about creating systems that bridge gaps and meet everyone's needs. You will see what I mean when we cover Communication and Expectations in Chapter 8, complete with data and client examples.

A New Path Forward: The Talent Impact Process

The Talent Impact Process is your playbook for navigating the shifting workplace landscape and reaching the Generational Advantage. This seven-step model brings clarity and structure to one of the most complex challenges leaders face today: building workplaces where all generations thrive and maximize their performance.

Here's what you can expect to learn by following the process throughout this book:

1. **Generational Excellence**—Understanding and leveraging the strengths of every generation
2. **Attraction**—Building employer brands that resonate across demographics
3. **Onboarding and Development**—Creating growth pathways for every employee
4. **Retention and Activation**—Activating potential while preventing burnout
5. **Communication and Expectations**—Aligning communication styles and setting clear goals
6. **Culture**—Cultivating values, behaviors, and actions that drive success
7. **Data**—Using insights to guide decision-making and prepare for the future

Each chapter in this book dives into one of the seven components of the Talent Impact Process, offering actionable insights, real-world examples, and practical tools you can implement immediately. Whether you're looking to transform your entire team or take small steps toward better alignment as an individual, this process is designed to meet you where you are. Remember, this isn't about checking off boxes or following rigid rules—it's about building a workplace where every generation feels valued, connected, and motivated to produce the results you need. No matter your role or experience level, if you're eager to learn and open to new ideas, this journey will equip you with the strategies to make meaningful, lasting change in your workforce.

About Our Research

Throughout this book, you'll see data from surveys and insights collected through my company, Generational Performance Solutions (GPS). Since 2018, we've gathered more than ten thousand responses from professionals across industries—including, but not limited to, finance, healthcare, construction, manufacturing, marketing, and nonprofit sectors. Our data comes from surveys shared on LinkedIn, live polling during keynote sessions, and direct distribution to our professional network, including both white-collar and blue-collar industries. These responses reflect a healthy mix of all working generations, giving us a real-time, cross-generational perspective on what employees want, need, and expect today.

While we don't position ourselves as a traditional research firm, we use this information to help leaders make smarter people decisions—and build workplaces where everyone, from Gen Z to Baby Boomers, can thrive.

Generational Harmony in Practice

I understand that generations are deeply personal, which is why you won't find stereotypes here or anywhere in my team's work. Instead, I'm focused on equipping you with actionable generational data to drive meaningful change. By leveraging these insights, your organization can strengthen communication, attract top talent, enhance retention, and drive engagement. Every generation brings unique strengths to the table, such as the following:

- Baby boomers bring experience and leadership, but they want to feel respected as they mentor others.
- Gen X leaders excel at bridging tradition with innovation (we call them the middle children of the generations), but they need tools to manage multigenerational teams.
- Millennials are driven by purpose and growth, but they want clear career paths.
- Gen Z brings fresh ideas and technological fluency, but they crave mentorship and connection.

The next wave—whether it's Generation Alpha today or Generation Beta in the future—will bring its own challenges and opportunities. Companies that act now to develop flexible and forward-thinking cultures that engage multigenerational talent will be best positioned to welcome them and set them up for success faster.

This book is not here to help you navigate today's challenges only—I'm really here to help build organizations that are ready for the future. Along the way, I will share real stories from companies that are getting it right (or wrong), data-backed strategies, and tools you can implement immediately.

Before diving into this book, it's important to acknowledge that we no longer live in a world where most people stay in one job for thirty years—like my parents, for example. Technology has made it easier than ever to explore new opportunities, and many organizations still struggle to focus on what truly drives long-term success: their people. The goal isn't to retain every employee for three decades, though that's great if you can. It's about creating environments where purpose, profitability, and performance are evident in your workplace. So instead of worrying about losing employees, ask yourself: What if you could retain top talent for three to five years? Think about the benefits—less time and money wasted on turnover, greater team stability, and the possibility of building strong alumni networks. A well-handled exit can even turn departing employees into future advocates or, better yet, boomerang talent who come back stronger and more experienced.

Now that you have a feel for what you're about to embark on, your journey starts here. Together, we'll explore how to align values, inspire stronger communication, and enhance workplaces where every generation can perform at the highest level, forming the Generational Advantage.

With this foundation in place, let's take a closer look at the challenges organizations are facing today—and why solving them requires a new approach. The next chapter will lay the groundwork for the solutions we'll explore together.

Are you ready to prepare for the future while honoring the traditions that have shaped your organization's past? Let's get started.

KEY TAKEAWAYS FROM CHAPTER 1:

- The modern workforce is made up of four active generations (which are constantly changing), and a shift requiring innovation and adaptability in communication, culture, and leadership is necessary.
- Flexibility, purpose-driven work, and clear communication are priorities across generations, but they must be tailored to individual needs to drive results.
- The Talent Impact Process is a seven-step playbook designed to help leaders create multigenerational workplaces where employees from all backgrounds thrive.

CHAPTER 2

THE CHALLENGES: GENERATIONAL GAPS IN TODAY'S WORKFORCE

Now that we've explored the generational shifts shaping today's workforce and those to come, let's confront a universal truth: Companies struggle to attract, retain, and develop talent long enough to see a true return on their investment. It doesn't matter whether they're working with young or experienced professionals—this is a challenge across the board.

So why is it so challenging to connect with the next generation and align across multiple age groups in the workplace? Good question. Let's unpack that a bit by identifying some of the major challenges organizations face today when it comes to their multigenerational workforces, which are filled with—you guessed it—*people*.

This chapter is designed to address the pressing workforce challenges your organization may be grappling with today. We'll identify these issues up front and provide a foundation for the solutions outlined in the following chapters. Through the lens of our process, you'll discover practical strategies to build a thriving multigenerational workforce. Let's begin by examining the most common obstacles you may already be facing.

1. The Financial Cost of Turnover
2. Bridging Generational Communication Gaps
3. Integrating New Generations Into Established Workplaces
4. Meeting Differing Demands and Expectations
5. The Unknowns of Gen Z and Beyond

THE COST OF TURNOVER

Annual Salary	1 Employee Leaving	5 Employees Leaving	10 Employees Leaving
$50,000	$25,000	$125,000	$250,000
$100,000	$100,000	$500,000	$1,000,000
$150,000	$300,000	$1,500,000	$3,000,000

Based on Gallup & BuiltIn estimates: turnover ranges from 0.5× to 2× salary depending on role and seniority.[6]

1. *The Financial Cost of Turnover*

The numbers don't lie. Studies consistently show that losing an employee within their first year costs businesses about half of that employee's annual salary. For instance, losing a team member with a $60,000 salary translates to $30,000 in recruiting fees, onboarding costs, and wasted training. This expense compounds further if you've partnered with a recruiting agency or invested heavily in specialized training.

But financial pain is just one part of the equation. High turnover also drains resources, destabilizes team dynamics, and leaves critical knowledge gaps within your workforce. And these challenges are often exacerbated in multigenerational teams when communication gaps, mismatched expectations, and resistance to change are present.

THE CHALLENGES: GENERATIONAL GAPS IN TODAY'S WORKFORCE

2. Bridging Generational Communication Gaps
One of the primary hurdles for multigenerational teams is communication—or, more specifically, miscommunication. Leaders often find that what worked for years with one group no longer resonates with younger employees, particularly Gen Z. This cohort grew up in a digital-first world dominated by social media, instant messaging (think Slack or Teams), and on-demand connectivity—or an "always on" society. As a result, they prefer direct, fast communication over lengthy emails or drawn-out face-to-face meetings.

But let's be clear: This doesn't mean Gen Z avoids in-person connection. In fact, they deeply value face-to-face interactions but only in environments that honor their need for flexibility and autonomy. I like to call this approach "on their own terms." Interestingly, after the isolation of the pandemic, many Gen Z professionals began actively seeking more interpersonal connection, even expressing a desire for in-office work. Why? Because some of them started their first and second jobs behind a camera. Many experienced college without ever stepping into a classroom or socializing beyond a Zoom screen. The difference now? They want the option for face-to-face engagement without the constraints of rigid, one-size-fits-all corporate structures. In other words, they want the face-to-face connection on their own terms (hybrid workplace has entered the chat).

On the flip side, older, more experienced generations may see Gen Z's reliance on technology as a lack of interpersonal skills, while Gen Z might view traditional communication methods as outdated or inefficient. These mismatched perspectives can (and do) lead to frustration, lowered connectivity, and, ultimately, higher turnover.

So how do you fix it?

- Start by promoting a culture of open communication that embraces varied preferences.

- Offer training that enhances digital fluency for seasoned employees while cultivating interpersonal skills for younger team members.
- Leverage collaboration tools like Slack, Teams, or Zoom that bridge communication styles effectively.
- Above all, set clear expectations about how your team will communicate—a solution I'll dive deeper into later in this book.

During a keynote I delivered last summer, a leader stood up and confidently declared, "When I call my young team member, I expect them to answer within ten minutes. If they don't return my call during working hours, that's grounds for termination."

I paused and asked, "Have you explicitly communicated this expectation to them?"

Without hesitation, he replied, "No, I don't need to. It's just common sense."

This response revealed a critical disconnect. After the session, we had a one-on-one conversation where I explained how failing to set clear expectations could alienate and ultimately drive away top talent. Once he understood the generational differences in communication styles and the need for explicit guidelines, he realized the importance of clarity for his current team and future workforce as well.

Here's the truth: What we often think of as common sense isn't common at all—it's shaped by our own experiences, assumptions, and generational norms. As leaders, clinging to the idea that the old way of doing things is the *only way* risks alienating top talent and creates a culture of frustration and misunderstanding. I understand that there is comfort in doing things the way you always have, but it is imperative that, as leaders (regardless of your role or title at work), you shift this type of thinking. If you want to lead a thriving multigenerational team that sees results, it's time to trade assumptions for clear communication and adaptability.

THE CHALLENGES: GENERATIONAL GAPS IN TODAY'S WORKFORCE

3. Integrating New Generations into Established Workplaces
At the time of writing this book, Gen Z is the new kid on the block, shaking up traditional workplaces. In five years, it will be Gen Alpha. Regardless of the cohort, newer generations tend to challenge long-standing workplace norms, creating friction in organizations slow to adapt. We must remind ourselves of this (yes, I am speaking to my millennial peers!). When we become the senior leaders of the workforce, we need to remember when baby boomers and others had our generation under a magnifying glass.

Gen Z, for example, prioritizes flexibility, autonomy, and meaningful work over the rigid hierarchies and fixed nine-to-five schedules of traditional corporate settings. They want to contribute from day one, feel valued, and have opportunities to grow. Environments that don't offer this risk losing them before their potential is realized.

A recent survey revealed that 73 percent of Gen Z professionals feel frustrated when their input is dismissed by more experienced colleagues.[7] Another says that one in five Gen Zers haven't had a single conversation with someone over fifty in their workplace in the last year.[8] How can we let this continue to happen in our workplaces? Meanwhile, older employees might perceive their newer counterparts as impatient or entitled, leading to unnecessary tension.

The solution lies in balance. Organizations can reconsider their work structures, incorporating flexibility through remote work options, adaptive schedules, or collaborative management styles. At the same time, integrating new hires with seasoned employees through mentorship programs promotes knowledge transfer and smoother transitions. While focusing on the incoming talent, it's equally crucial to support long-tenured employees. Change can be unsettling, and sidelining experienced staff in favor of newcomers only creates more resistance.

History shows us that generational tension is cyclical. Every wave of workers faces skepticism as they step into the workforce, only to later become the old guard wary of the next generation. Understanding this pattern allows leaders to approach these shifts with empathy and foresight instead of resistance. By striking the right balance, organizations can create workplaces where all generations contribute, advance, and grow together. This is the Generational Advantage in action.

When people ask about the ultimate goal of Generational Performance Solutions, my answer is always clear: Success means breaking the generational cycle of dismissing the new kids on the block. Picture a future where Gen Z rises to leadership without perpetuating the same biases—where they greet the next wave of talent (whatever name they may hold) with curiosity and respect, valuing their unique contributions rather than fixating on their differences. This isn't just about being generationally inclusive for the sake of it. It's about building stronger teams, increasing productivity, and making work actually work. When people aren't stuck battling generational friction, they spend more time doing great work. And when that happens, results take care of themselves.

I have been fortunate to meet many leaders over the last decade who already embody this forward-thinking mentality, leaders who see value in bridging generational divides and championing the strengths of every employee. However, the reality is that not all leaders share this same mindset. Let's continue to push for a workplace where all leaders embrace this mindset, shaping environments that are built on respect, understanding, and shared purpose.

If we can establish environments that prioritize mutual respect and understanding over generational stereotypes, then we'll have redefined what's possible for the workforce. That's the legacy we should all strive for.

4. *Meeting Differing Demands and Expectations*
As a business leader, you might understandably be overwhelmed by having to contend with these complex multigenerational dynamics

on top of everything else you need to stay ahead of with work. It's no secret that generational priorities vary widely. For instance:

- Gen Z: Values purpose-driven work, company transparency, and career growth opportunities. They'll leave quickly if their expectations aren't met.
- Millennials: Often bridge generations, valuing flexibility, work-life balance, and meaningful career development. While labeled the "job-hopping generation," millennials often leave jobs due to stagnation or misaligned values, not lack of loyalty.
- Gen X: Values independence, flexibility, and financial stability, often serving as team stabilizers.
- Baby Boomers: Seek security and value their workplace tenure as a marker of loyalty and dedication.

The challenge is that younger employees, especially Gen Z and younger millennials, are much quicker to leave a role that doesn't meet their standards compared to more experienced generations. We've seen that this does not even change much in an employer-driven job market. They're drawn to and stay with companies that have strong values, visible commitments to social and environmental causes, and clear career paths.

To meet these expectations:

1. Strengthen your employer brand by communicating your company's values clearly and ensuring your actions match your messaging.
2. Offer continuous learning opportunities! Young employees want growth, so invest in robust training and development programs to maximize their performance.
3. Be transparent by providing regular feedback and clear career pathways that will help your employees feel valued and give them direction.

Rather than viewing the next generation as a challenge to accommodate, think of them as a powerful asset. When you tap into their potential and align their motivations with your business goals, you unlock fresh energy, innovation, and long-term success.

5. *The Unknowns of Gen Z (and Beyond)*
Perhaps the biggest challenge for today's leaders is the uncertainty surrounding Gen Z's long-term behavior in the workforce. This is a generation that adapts quickly and values change, but it's also still defining itself, much like the next generation (and the one after that) will need to define itself. Their career preferences and patterns are still emerging, leaving organizations grappling with how to best attract and retain them.

For example, their comfort with technology is a strength, but it also raises expectations, not to mention skepticism (dubbed the "Anxious Generation,"[9] they entered the workforce under a magnifying glass). Companies must adopt cutting-edge tools and practices to keep up. Similarly, their openness to frequent job changes may frustrate organizations seeking long-term stability.

Another layer of complexity? Technology is evolving faster than most workplaces can adapt—and artificial intelligence (AI) is at the center of it all. Gen Z is already working alongside AI tools in ways that redefine what "productive" looks like, and future generations will only deepen that integration. While older employees may view AI with skepticism or caution, younger talent tends to see it as a collaborative partner—a tool that enhances creativity, streamlines tasks, and opens the door to new possibilities. The challenge isn't whether to adopt AI—it's how to adopt it in a way that empowers every generation to thrive. Leaders must encourage a culture where technological learning is ongoing, not intimidating, and where cross-generational teams can explore how to apply tools like AI without widening generational gaps.

THE CHALLENGES: GENERATIONAL GAPS IN TODAY'S WORKFORCE

How can leaders navigate this uncertainty?

First, you can stay informed on emerging trends and conduct regular feedback sessions with employees to anticipate their evolving needs, which can help you maximize their performance. After that, it's a good idea to create dynamic, adaptable workplaces that cater to both short-term wins and long-term growth.

Moving Forward with Generational Understanding

High turnover does more than just cost money—it disrupts morale, drains resources, and hinders growth. But this isn't a new problem. For centuries, workplaces have faced tension between the old guard and the new wave. The difference today is our ability to anticipate generational shifts and proactively prepare for them.

At its core, generational understanding is the awareness of the behaviors, values, and work preferences shaped by each generation's unique experiences. It focuses on recognizing and respecting these differences to improve communication and collaboration. Unlike the Generational Advantage, which emphasizes leveraging these differences to gain a competitive edge, generational understanding is about encouraginging empathy and inclusivity within the workforce. When you practice generational understanding, you can adapt quickly to the rapidly changing workforce. We'll cover how you can do this in Chapter 4 when I walk you through the first step of the Talent Impact Process: Generational Excellence.

Books like *The Fourth Turning* by Neil Howe and William Strauss highlight the predictable cycles of generational archetypes throughout history. Understanding these patterns can give leaders a roadmap for managing change. Instead of reacting to generational shifts with frustration, we really can—and should—embrace them with confidence and adaptability. It will only make our workplaces and homes more effective.

If you're a leader reading this, you likely have felt some of the pains I have addressed above. While I provided a few steps that you can initially take in this chapter, the following pages will provide deeper solutions and action steps for your teams to take if you want to prepare for the future of your workforce.

By the end of this book, you'll have a comprehensive strategy to overcome workplace challenges, harness generational diversity, and create an environment where every age group thrives and is motivated in their respective roles. In the next chapter, we'll explore how to build a generationally aligned engine tailored to your unique organization.

> *Dive deeper with your downloadable worksheet and apply what you've learned right away. Visit:*
> https://thegenerationaladvantage.com/get-downloads/

THE CHALLENGES: GENERATIONAL GAPS IN TODAY'S WORKFORCE

KEY TAKEAWAYS FROM CHAPTER 2:

- Turnover is one of the costliest challenges for organizations today. High employee attrition drains morale, destabilizes teams, and results in significant financial losses, but it is preventable with intentional strategies.

- Miscommunication across generations creates frustration, reduces connectivity, and drives turnover. Bridging these gaps through open communication, training, and clear expectations is essential for success.

- Generational priorities vary, but flexibility, autonomy, and alignment with personal values are emerging as universal expectations in today's workforce.

- Adapting to the unknowns of Gen Z and future generations will require continuous learning, proactive planning, and a commitment to creating dynamic workplaces that meet the needs of all employees.

CHAPTER 3

THE TALENT IMPACT PROCESS: A NEW ERA OF WORKFORCE STRATEGY

Now that we've identified the major challenges faced by today's workplaces, let's shift our focus to the solution—a proven framework that transforms organizations into thriving, multigenerational ecosystems. What does this transformation look like? Enhanced profit, performance, productivity, and credibility. Where does it begin? Right here.

The GPS Talent Impact Process is built upon seven game-changing elements that together form a comprehensive cross-generational talent strategy and playbook. Like any well-designed process, it requires commitment and patience. You can't skip ahead to results; real, sustainable change takes time.

Since we developed this proprietary process, over two thousand organizations have implemented this tool and witnessed its transformative impact. Now, it's your turn to join them.

The formula is straightforward yet powerful:

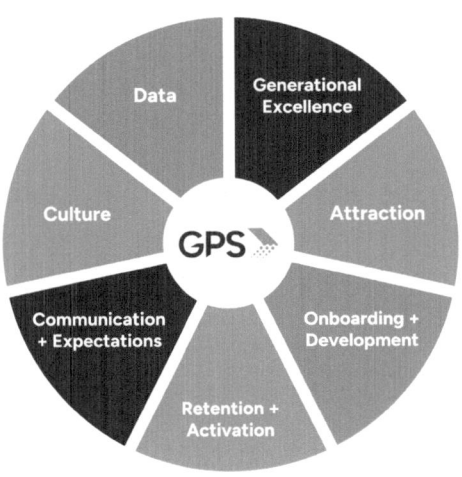

The Seven Elements of the Talent Impact Process

1. Generational Excellence
Success begins with understanding and valuing the unique contributions of every generation. Each age group brings its own strengths, preferences, and perspectives to the table, and leveraging these differences creates a high-functioning, inclusive workplace.

In Chapter 4, we'll explore questions such as:

- *How can your organization support ongoing generational training and safe spaces for open discussion?*
- *How well are generational tensions addressed—or avoided altogether?*

Generational Excellence is the foundation of the process and the first step because without it, the rest of the wheel falters.

2. Attraction

Attracting a multigenerational talent pool starts with an authentic brand, both online and in person. Your employer brand must resonate across all generations. Are you speaking *to* the talent you want, or are you unintentionally excluding certain age groups through outdated or one-dimensional strategies?

In Chapter 5, we'll challenge you to evaluate:

- *How are your practices of social media, websites, and communication engaging a multigenerational audience authentically?*
- *How can your recruitment strategy reach candidates across multiple backgrounds?*

Organizations that intentionally create hiring processes welcome to all generations will see broader, more sustainable results.

3. Onboarding and Development

A strong start can mean the difference between retention and turnover. Effective onboarding and continuous development build clarity, confidence, and trust regardless of age.

We'll tackle critical questions in Chapter 6 such as:

- *Is your onboarding process clear, welcoming, and tailored for success?*
- *Do you provide pathways for ongoing growth and development that resonate with employees across generations?*

Development matters to every age group. Aligning expectations and harnessing growth ensures long-term success.

4. Retention and Activation

Keeping employees engaged and inspired is not optional—it's essential. Retention is more than keeping bodies in seats; it's about activating potential to maximize productivity. Employees should feel that their careers are defined, fulfilling, and supported. When employees—regardless of generation—understand their roles, feel challenged, and see clear career paths, they perform better. This isn't about "making them happy"—it's about reducing unnecessary turnover and ensuring you get a return on your investment in their training.

Key areas we'll address in Chapter 7 include:

- *What steps can you take to tailor your engagement strategies to generational preferences?*
- *How can you create rewards and recognition systems that resonate across all age groups?*

Retention rates increase when organizations commit to well-being, clarity, and purpose for every generation.

5. Communication and Expectations

Clear communication builds trust, aligns expectations, and bridges generational divides. In a multigenerational workplace, communication isn't one size fits all; it must be intentional, flexible, and inclusive.

In Chapter 8, we'll explore:

- *How can you tailor your communication to reach different generations effectively?*
- *Are you aligning goals and expectations clearly for all age groups?*

The most successful organizations know that effective communication goes beyond talking and is all about connection.

6. Culture

A thriving culture doesn't happen by accident. It's created through intention, consistency, and authenticity. Do you offer a flexible, supportive environment that lives up to its values?

We'll consider questions in Chapter 9 such as:

- *What actions can you take to create a generationally inclusive culture, and does it inadvertently exclude or overwhelm certain groups?*
- *What methods could you use to encourage mental health, flexibility, and work-life balance without judgment?*

A strong culture attracts, retains, and inspires. It creates a workplace where people—across all generations—feel they belong.

7. Data

The workplace is evolving rapidly, and the organizations that will flourish are the ones that think forward and embrace change. Backed by data, you'll be able to make informed, strategic decisions that drive results.

In Chapter 10, we'll dive into:

- *How can you use data to measure the effectiveness of your generational strategies?*
- *What methods can you use to ensure you are prepared for emerging workforce shifts, such as AI and its impact on future generations?*

Data transforms guesswork into strategy. By understanding where you stand today, you'll know exactly how to shape your workplace for tomorrow.

Bringing It All Together

The Talent Impact Process is not only a framework; it's a roadmap for your cross-generational transformation. As you look at the playbook, remember that the process works best when implemented in order. Skipping ahead may be tempting—after all, attraction and retention are where most leaders want to focus—but without Generational Excellence as your foundation, the results won't stick.

The GPS team is actively applying our own Talent Impact Process every day, so we are right here with you. We continually assess our growing team to ensure we're living out the very principles we advocate. This commitment is evident in how we hire, onboard, retain, and communicate with the talent that joins our team, and we've learned some hard lessons that I will outline in the pages ahead. Here's an important truth: The Talent Impact Process is never truly finished. It's a journey of ongoing improvement, adapting to evolving teams and shifting generational dynamics.

In the coming chapters, I will break down each element of the process in detail, offering real-world examples from organizations that have adopted the Talent Impact Process and reaped the rewards. By the end of this book, you'll have the tools, strategies, and insights needed to create a workplace where all generations thrive and your organization's goals are met.

Dive deeper with your downloadable worksheet and apply what you've learned right away. Visit: https://thegenerationaladvantage.com/get-downloads/

To deepen your understanding and help you take immediate action, each chapter will include links to online resources, including quizzes, activities, and implementation guides. These tools are designed to complement the lessons in the book and make the Talent Impact Process accessible to organizations of all sizes.

Finally, keep this in mind as you move forward: This is not just about understanding the next generation of workers. The Talent Impact Process is about building workplaces where all generations prosper together, learning from one another's strengths and bridging divides. As you explore these pages, approach the ideas with an open mind, and challenge yourself to apply these strategies across your entire team—not just the youngest or newest members. By embracing a cross-generational perspective, you'll create a workplace where every individual feels valued and motivated to contribute to your organization's success, which will have maximum impact on your purpose, performance, and profitability.

Let's start at the beginning: Generational Excellence.

KEY TAKEAWAYS FROM CHAPTER 3:

- The Talent Impact Process is a comprehensive seven-step framework designed to align generational understanding with actionable strategies, ensuring your organization thrives in today's multigenerational workforce.

- Success begins with Generational Excellence—the foundation of the process. By understanding and embracing the unique contributions of each generation, organizations can create workplaces where collaboration and respect yield results.

- The Talent Impact Process is a roadmap that empowers leaders to create adaptable, future-focused workplaces that attract, engage, and retain top talent across all generations.

CHAPTER 4

GENERATIONAL EXCELLENCE: BUILDING BRIDGES

You may be wondering, "What does Generational Excellence even mean?" Generational Excellence means creating a workplace where all generations are aware of, understand, and respect each other's differences and similarities. It's about recognizing where people come from—whether it's their upbringings, formative historical moments, or cultural influences—and using this understanding to build stronger, more high-performing teams.

In our philosophy, Generational Excellence is the single most critical factor that ensures your profitability and credibility remain strong and that your organization's legacy continues long after your leadership tenure.

The reality is: Most organizations lack generational awareness, let alone Generational Excellence. Think of it as the *ultimate goal and generational awareness as one of the first steps to getting there.*

How Do You Achieve Generational Excellence?

To build a workplace where all generations thrive, we focus on five actionable pillars:

1. Training: Building the Foundation
2. Awareness: Cultivating Generational Mindfulness
3. Communication: Bridging Generational Gaps
4. Engagement: Turning Awareness into Action
5. Leadership: Modeling Generational Excellence

Let's begin with the first component: training.

1. Training: Building the Foundation

Training is where Generational Excellence begins. It's about creating a baseline understanding of the strengths and preferences of every generation. But what sets this apart: Our programs don't just highlight differences—we emphasize the synergies. After all, understanding the individual *behind* the label is more important than relying on broad generational stereotypes.

In a Generational Excellence training, we cover:

- **Generational Characteristics:** A thoughtful look at what defines each generation—from baby boomers to Gen Alpha—without overgeneralizing.
- **Communication Styles:** We break through stereotypes (like: not all baby boomers love face-to-face meetings, and not all Gen Z members are glued to TikTok) and emphasize data-driven methods to understand how your employees want to communicate.
- **Conflict Resolution:** Breaking down generational conflict is essential. Despite popular belief, we're not as different

as we often believe. Most people are shocked when I recommend setting aside rigid generational data to focus on managing individuals. Why? Because, at the end of the day, we are more than the generation we were born into—we're unique people with distinct preferences. Generational data is a powerful tool for understanding trends and communication styles, but it's not the whole story. For example, a baby boomer might be more comfortable texting than their Gen Z colleague, despite the stereotype. Our training equips teams to see beyond these labels, building understanding and collaboration based on who people truly are, not just when they were born.

Depending on your company's size and available resources, we recommend partnering with a third party to train your team for maximum impact. Our workshops—which we highlight below through a real-time case study—are built on this framework and consistently achieve a 100 percent satisfaction rate. Alternatively, you can empower your internal team to lead these trainings, but keep in mind that the framework may need to be adapted to fit your specific context and industry.

> **Case Study: Bridging Gaps at a Small Architecture Firm**
> In one of our most impactful workshops, we partnered with a boutique architecture firm that had a mix of millennial architects, Gen X managers, and baby boomer partners to tackle long-standing intergenerational tensions. These challenges had quietly simmered for years, impacting collaboration and productivity. The core issue? Misaligned perspectives on technology and tradition. The baby boomer architects harbored frustration watching millennials rely on tools like CAD and Revit, feeling that these advancements overlooked the craftsmanship and effort of traditional hand-drafting

that they experienced for much of their early careers. Meanwhile, the millennial team members were oblivious to the historical struggles of sketching for hours at drafting tables and viewed their methods as outdated.

Our three-hour Intergenerational Communication Workshop opened with a quick recap of the barriers and generational insights you just read about. From there, we moved straight into hands-on application of the Talent Impact Process (TIP). Through exercises and small breakout groups, employees used the seven-step TIP framework to see issues from each other's perspective and agree on concrete next steps.

While a single workshop couldn't resolve all the tensions, it was a turning point. Team members openly acknowledged frustrations and discovered unexpected areas of mutual respect. For instance, baby boomers gained an appreciation for the efficiency tools millennials brought to the table, while millennials developed a newfound respect for the artistry and dedication of traditional drafting techniques. Over time, generational shifts will bring new differences to the table, but this framework will stay the same.

The Results:
- **Improved Collaboration**: By creating a dialogue, the firm's teams began to work together more fluidly, leveraging both modern tools and traditional methods.
- **Stronger Culture**: Regular follow-ups, including quarterly check-ins, further strengthened the culture of communication and collaboration.
- **Sustained Growth**: The firm reported an increase in project efficiency and employee satisfaction within the first six months of implementing these changes.

Generational training is just the start. True transformation requires ongoing strategies, consistent follow-ups, and a willingness to adapt. For this architecture firm, investing in their team's understanding of each other was the blueprint for a more harmonious and innovative future, and I've seen the same results countless times with other organizations that adopted this approach.

2. Awareness: Cultivating Generational Mindfulness
Awareness goes hand in hand with training, building on a workplace culture where employees actively recognize and value generational diversity. It starts with small intentional practices that build bridges between different age groups. For example, pairing younger employees with seasoned professionals can create opportunities for mutual learning and knowledge sharing, helping both sides grow in unexpected ways. Similarly, adopting inclusive policies—like offering caregiving benefits or flexible schedules for varying life stages—ensures all generations feel supported in the workplace.

Leaders play a vital role in setting the tone for generational awareness. Their decisions and daily interactions should reflect respect for unique perspectives. Recognizing the contributions of all generations through storytelling, awards, or events reinforces a sense of belonging and celebrates the richness of a multigenerational team.

I know there are possibly some leaders who believe that focusing on generational inclusion adds unnecessary complexity to the workplace. However, overlooking these dynamics often results in missed opportunities for stronger collaboration, improved performance, and deeper employee engagement. When leaders actively acknowledge and support generational differences, they create environments where individuals feel seen, heard, and motivated to contribute their best.

3. Communication: Bridging Generational Gaps
Communication is the backbone of Generational Excellence, yet it's often the source of misunderstandings. Clear, respectful dialogue helps bridge gaps and dispel assumptions. Different generations may prefer distinct modes of communication—some lean toward email, while others gravitate toward instant messaging or collaborative tools. By providing a mix of channels and encouraging open discussions in roundtables or cross-generational teams, organizations create pathways for connection and trust.

Constructive feedback is another cornerstone of effective communication. It's essential to deliver feedback in ways that respect individual sensitivities while maintaining clarity. Entry-level team members, for instance, should feel safe voicing their opinions without fear of judgment. If they don't, you might miss out on some valuable insights from a different demographic that will impact the future of your workforce. Look at it this way: Your future clients are members of the next generation, so it's valuable to at least consider their opinions when looking at it from a client or vendor perspective.

By cultivating this level of inclusivity, organizations unlock fresh perspectives and valuable insights from younger employees, which drives collaboration across the board.

4. Engagement: Turning Awareness into Action
Engagement takes generational awareness to the next level, transforming understanding into tangible impact. When employees feel genuinely invested, they naturally curate a culture of respect, collaboration, and shared purpose. For example, organizing cross-generational team projects or workshops can break down barriers and highlight the strengths of different age groups working together.

Recognizing contributions is another key component of engagement. Acknowledging the achievements of employees—whether they're at the start of their career or nearing retirement—creates a sense of value and belonging. At the same time, career development opportunities tailored to individual needs help employees see a future within the organization. Mentorship programs and structured growth pathways ensure that every team member feels supported and encouraged to reach their potential. We will come back to this topic in Chapter 6.

5. Leadership: Modeling Generational Excellence
Generational Excellence excels under leadership that sets the tone for connection and collaboration. Leaders have the unique responsibility to bridge divides, inspire connection, and champion inclusion across all generations. This begins with modeling respect in daily interactions—whether it's showing patience when introducing new tools or valuing the insights of both seasoned professionals and newer hires.

True leaders also guide by example, mentoring across generations and encouraging an environment where everyone learns from one another. Articulating a clear vision for Generational Excellence and embedding it into the organization's strategy ensures that this mindset becomes part of the workplace DNA. By doing so, leaders not only create a cohesive culture today but also lay the foundation for a stronger, more unified workforce in the future.

Be a Proactive Leader Using Generational Excellence

Think of the Generational Excellence pillars outlined above as your roadmap to building a strong foundation for achieving workforce success. Imagine driving results by setting a new standard for leadership—one that prioritizes connection, collaboration, and innovation. Many leaders today lack these essentials in their toolkit, which presents you with an opportunity to lead differently and stay ahead of the curve! Challenges like communication breakdowns and the struggle to attract and retain top talent in a post-pandemic labor market demand a proactive approach but are often met with watered-down solutions. Instead of reacting to changes, take control. By prioritizing Generational Excellence, you create the groundwork for effective hiring, onboarding, and retention. This approach strengthens communication, sets clear expectations, promotes an inclusive culture, and empowers your organization with actionable insights through data. Be the leader who changes the game, not the one who's forced to adapt.

As you reflect on the steps in this chapter, ask yourself: How is my organization turning awareness into action? Are we creating opportunities for cross-generational collaboration, recognizing contributions in meaningful ways, and modeling the behaviors we want to see? If your organization is already practicing Generational Excellence, kudos to you. If not, know that you will be soon. Just follow the process and steps below, and you'll be well on your way.

KEY TAKEAWAYS FROM CHAPTER 4:

- Creating a workplace where all generations understand, respect, and leverage each other's unique contributions ensures long-term success, profitability, and legacy.
- Generational Excellence begins with training that highlights the similarities between generations, focusing on individuals rather than stereotypes.
- Clear, intentional communication using multiple channels and safe forums for feedback bridges generational gaps and prevents misunderstandings.
- Leaders who model respect, provide mentorship, and articulate a vision for generational collaboration ensure the success of Generational Excellence initiatives.

Before wrapping up, let's translate what you've learned into immediate, actionable steps. Each chapter outlining the Talent Impact Process comes with clear next steps and additional resources, which you can explore online. Since we know not all readers prefer to view their information online, there are downloadable PDFs that you can print as well!

 Your Next Steps

1. **Assign Responsibility:** Identify who will oversee Generational Excellence at the beginning—whether it's HR, a task force, or a senior leader. Ideally, this eventually becomes everyone, but for now, create a plan for the beginning.
2. **Schedule Your First Generational Training Session:** Whether you choose to partner with an experienced facilitator, a respected internal leader, or an outside expert, the important thing is to start. There are many credible organizations leading this work—each with different approaches and strengths. If you're looking for a place to begin, Generational Performance Solutions offers customized training sessions rooted in real-world data and team dynamics. Contact us at information@genperformance.com to learn more.
3. **Commit to Ongoing Action:** Use the Generational Excellence framework to set measurable goals, track progress, and maintain momentum.

If you embrace these steps, you'll be ready for whatever transformations Gen Z, Gen Alpha, and beyond bring to the workforce. I'm often asked, "Kamber, how will you continue serving clients as the workforce evolves?" My answer is simple: Generational Excellence ensures I'm always learning, always engaging, and always growing. By embracing this process, your organization—and its legacy—will achieve lasting impact.

Now that you've laid the groundwork for Generational Excellence, it's time to focus on Step 2: Attraction. In the next chapter, we'll explore how to create a compelling employer brand and recruit talent across all generations—strategies that ensure you bring the right people into your organization through generationally conscious strategies.

> Dive deeper with your downloadable worksheet and apply what you've learned right away. Visit:
> https://thegenerationaladvantage.com/get-downloads/

CHAPTER 5

ATTRACTING TALENT: CREATING A MAGNETIC BRAND

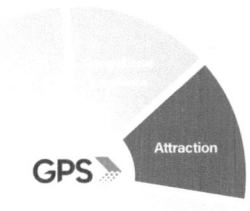

Now that you've set the foundation of Generational Excellence, it's time to address the second piece of the GPS Talent Impact Process: attracting multigenerational talent.

Once leadership is aligned and generational awareness is established, you're ready to implement the right strategies to attract top talent across all generations. In this chapter, we'll break this step into five focus areas that will set your organization apart:

1. Digital Branding and Execution
2. Building a Strategy
3. Authenticity: Selling Your Culture, Not Your Services
4. Setting Up Hiring for Success
5. Strong Recruiting = Strong Retention

Each section will include real-world examples, practical tips, and actionable steps to help you level up your recruiting game with the Generational Advantage in mind. While my team doesn't specialize in direct recruitment, we collaborate closely with trusted recruiting partners and focus on equipping organizations with the strategies and best practices needed to navigate today's complex hiring landscape effectively. This chapter will empower you to attract and secure the best talent across all generations.

1. Digital Branding and Execution
In the modern workforce, your candidates' first impressions of your organization start online.

Before they apply, job seekers will visit your website, social media platforms, and online reviews to understand your brand. They want to understand your culture, values, and what makes your organization a great place to work. At GPS, our research shows that 70 percent of young professionals will check a company's social media presence on channels like TikTok, Instagram, or YouTube before applying. Experienced generations do the same, though not nearly as much as young talent, and typically through platforms like LinkedIn or Facebook.

Understanding where your audience spends their time online is key to targeting them effectively. Research from Pew indicates that 95 percent of Gen Z is active on YouTube, with 67 percent on TikTok and 62 percent on Instagram, making these platforms essential for reaching younger candidates.[10] Millennials, on the other hand, maintain a strong presence on Instagram (71 percent), Facebook (70 percent), and LinkedIn (41 percent), often using these networks for both social and professional engagement.

For Gen X, 77 percent use Facebook regularly, while 91 percent engage with YouTube, and nearly half (48 percent) use Instagram. Meanwhile, baby boomers are most active on Facebook (73 percent) and YouTube (83 percent), though some also use platforms like Pinterest (38 percent) for industry-related content.

Not knowing where your audience lives online can be a huge challenge, especially in industries like manufacturing and construction. When we first connect with these organizations, they often struggle to attract younger workers. A quick glance at their social media often reveals the problem: Many rely solely on Facebook. Knowing that Gen Z overwhelmingly gravitates toward platforms like Instagram, YouTube, and TikTok, we often recommend diversifying their digital strategy to effectively connect with this new generation of talent.

> **Case Study: How a Construction Firm Revamped Its Digital Recruiting Strategy**
>
> A midsize construction firm partnered with us to overhaul their digital recruiting strategy. They had been relying solely on Facebook to connect with candidates but were struggling to attract Gen Z workers. Based on our insights, we knew that Gen Z was unlikely to engage on Facebook and recommended expanding their digital presence to align with the platforms where their target candidates were most active.
>
> Working together, we developed a strategy tailored to their multigenerational candidate pool. LinkedIn and Facebook remained the focus for seasoned professionals, while Instagram and YouTube were introduced to reach younger candidates through engaging video content. The results were transformative:
>
> - **725 percent growth** in careers page traffic from social media as campaigns successfully funneled candidates from posts to their website
> - **63 percent increase** in overall social media engagement, with content highlighting employee stories and company culture

> The lesson? Success comes from knowing where your audience lives online and crafting the right story to connect with them. By showcasing your team, their accomplishments, and your company culture, you can stand out as an employer of choice for all generations.

Our team has experienced tremendous success leveraging online platforms for hiring. For example, our director of operations, who oversees HR functions including recruitment, often shares that a single hiring post on our GPS LinkedIn page can generate twenty-plus resumes. This simple yet effective strategy has proven to be a powerful tool for attracting top talent when utilized thoughtfully.

2. Building a Strategy
An effective hiring strategy prioritizes meaningful connections with candidates who align with your organization's culture, values, and long-term goals—not just filling roles. To do this effectively, you need to create a consistent, compelling message that integrates branding with recruiting. It starts with understanding exactly who you're trying to attract. What drives them? What are their priorities, pain points, and aspirations?

Once you've identified your audience, the next step is crafting a message that speaks directly to them. Are they looking for growth opportunities, a supportive team culture, or greater flexibility? Highlight what makes your organization stand out in these areas. For example, if innovation is at the heart of your company, your messaging should showcase how employees are empowered to think creatively and contribute meaningfully.

The platforms you use also matter. As noted earlier in the chapter, younger candidates may gravitate toward Instagram or TikTok, where they can see behind-the-scenes glimpses of your culture, while seasoned professionals might be more engaged on a traditional professional platform like LinkedIn. Being intentional about where and how you share your story ensures your efforts resonate with the right audience.

During one of our focus groups, a young professional shared her job search journey, narrowing her options to three companies. All of them had vibrant social media channels celebrating team milestones, professional development, and employee recognition. She felt connected to their cultures before even applying. Meanwhile, companies without a strong online presence weren't even considered. This is the reality of the younger workforce and one that I encourage you to come to terms with. It doesn't have to be a bad thing for your team, though. You can leverage this information, which I encourage you to do!

This story illustrates the shift we're seeing in the job market today. Candidates are drawn to organizations that align with their values and communicate those values effectively. When you build a tailored strategy that reflects the priorities of your ideal candidates, you not only increase engagement but also attract individuals who will excel within your organization.

3. Authenticity: Selling Your Culture, Not Your Services
Your culture is not solely what you promote online; it's how you show up every day in your workplace. If your external messaging promises collaboration and inclusivity, your internal reality needs to deliver on that promise. In other words, what you do matters as much as you say. Younger hires, especially Gen Z, quickly notice when actions don't align with words.

When we work with clients, we take a deep dive into their branding and employee feedback. We cross-check their LinkedIn posts, Glassdoor reviews, and direct employee input via surveys to ensure that the message they're projecting online matches the day-to-day experience of their team. Why? Because candidates aren't shy about calling out discrepancies. If they sense a disconnect between your stated culture and your actual practices, trust is broken. Worse, negative reviews and disengaged candidates can harm your recruiting efforts for years to come.

> **Case Study: Humanizing the Brand—A Financial Firm's Cultural Shift**
> Take, for example, a financial services client we worked with. Initially, their online presence focused on "polished perfection"—formal team photos, overly curated posts, and staged office settings. It looked professional but lacked relatability. We encouraged them to take a different approach: showcasing team members in action, celebrating mentorship successes, and highlighting professional milestones. They began posting stories of individual wins, casual team gatherings, and behind-the-scenes moments. The shift was noteworthy. Candidates felt a more genuine connection to the company's values, resulting in increased applications and, more importantly, stronger retention. We'll get to more tips for retention in Chapter 7.

The lesson here is simple but powerful: Let your people and their stories represent your culture. Share moments that reflect the heartbeat of your organization, from volunteer initiatives to diversity efforts to everyday celebrations.

> **Case Study: Recruiting Through Relatable Moments**
> One of my favorite examples of this comes from an engineering firm we have worked with for several years. Behind their building, they had a basketball court where employees often played during breaks. When we first started working with them, we encouraged

> their team to share a candid action shot of one of their partners leaping while shooting a three-pointer—a moment of lighthearted fun that was anything but polished or staged. Though hesitant at first, the team agreed, and the post went live. The result? A surge of engagement (and maybe a couple of laughs), showcasing a culture that was dynamic, relatable, and real.

Authenticity does not equate to perfection—it means transparency. When candidates see that, they start imagining a long-term future with your organization—not just another job.

4. Setting Up Hiring for Success
Building a strong hiring pipeline ensures long-term success, especially when viewed through a multigenerational lens. It's time to think outside the box—hiring today looks vastly different than it used to, and so do the methods you need to use. Start by proactively sourcing candidates through platforms like LinkedIn, job boards, and social media. Don't overlook established channels like YouTube and, with respect to its future, TikTok, which is gaining traction for creative roles and younger candidates.

Engaging with your audience is equally important. Use interactive content such as polls, Q&A sessions, and behind-the-scenes videos to create connections with potential candidates long before roles even open. At the same time, streamline your application process to make it as simple and mobile-friendly as possible—complicated applications often drive top talent away. This has been an incredibly engaging way to connect with our audience and talent pipeline at GPS, so don't underestimate the power of these tools for your organization!

Finally, invest in developing your hiring team. Train recruiters to use the latest tools and techniques, including AI-powered recruitment technologies, to ensure they're staying ahead of trends. A forward-thinking approach will give your organization a competitive edge and help you attract a strong multigenerational talent pool. The next decade will bring the rise of the "Talent Marketing Specialist" role, so don't be the last one to integrate this function into your organization.

5. Strong Recruiting = Strong Retention
Recruiting and retention are two sides of the same coin. When you attract candidates who genuinely align with your company's culture and values, they are far more likely to stay, progress, and contribute meaningfully to your success. On the other hand, poor recruiting practices often result in disengaged employees and higher turnover rates, leading to sunk costs.

To strengthen both recruiting and retention, start by focusing on cultural fit during recruitment. Hiring people whose personal values and goals align with your mission creates a foundation for long-term engagement. Equally important is creating an exceptional candidate experience—those first interactions set the tone for how employees perceive your organization in the long run. Additionally, don't underestimate the power of your existing team. Engaged employees naturally become advocates for your brand, sharing their positive experiences and drawing like-minded talent to your organization.

Generational data can be a valuable tool in this stage of the Talent Impact Process, but it's crucial to remember that people are more than the generations they belong to—they are individuals with unique skills, perspectives, and needs. Recruiting effectively means seeing them as such. While the principles outlined above provide a solid foundation, success comes from balancing the generational lens with a personalized, human-centered approach to attract the right talent for your organization.

ATTRACTING TALENT: CREATING A MAGNETIC BRAND

> **KEY TAKEAWAYS FROM CHAPTER 5:**
>
> - A strong digital presence is crucial for the next wave of generational marketing—but different generations use different platforms. Craft tailored messaging to meet candidates where they are, whether through LinkedIn for experienced professionals or TikTok for younger job seekers.
> - Modern hiring requires modern strategies. Staying ahead of trends, such as leveraging emerging platforms or using AI-powered recruitment tools, ensures you attract the best-fit candidates in today's competitive landscape.
> - Clear, intentional communication using multiple channels and safe forums for feedback bridges generational gaps and prevents misunderstandings.
> - Engaged employees are your best advocates. When your current team is satisfied and aligned with your mission, they naturally promote your brand and attract like-minded talent.

Before wrapping up this chapter, let's translate what you've learned into immediate, actionable steps. Ready to elevate your talent attraction strategy?

Your Next Steps

1. **Assemble a Task Force:** Bring together HR and marketing team members to collaborate on your recruiting strategy.
2. **Audit Your Current Digital Presence:** What's working? What's not? Document the gaps and opportunities.
3. **Develop a Digital Media Plan:** Focus on recruiting, development, and retention. If you're looking for a partner to work alongside you, our advising services offer digital media strategies that emphasize attracting talent first. For more information, email <u>workwithus@genperformance.com.</u>
4. **Start Small, Think Big:** Begin with simple posts highlighting team achievements, values, and culture. Build from there.

> **PRO TIP**: Stay patient. A robust recruiting strategy takes time to produce results, but when done intentionally, it transforms both attraction and retention.

Dive deeper with your downloadable worksheet and apply what you've learned right away. Visit:
https://thegenerationaladvantage.com/get-downloads/

If you've made it this far, congratulations—you're already a few steps into creating a thriving multigenerational workplace. By focusing on attracting talent with authenticity and strategy, you'll build the foundation for success.

In the next chapter, we'll tackle Step 3 of the GPS Talent Impact Process: Onboarding and Development—the key to retaining and activating your new hires. Let's keep going.

CHAPTER 6

ONBOARDING AND DEVELOPMENT REIMAGINED

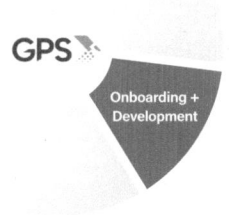

Attracting the right talent is just the first step. But what happens once they join your organization? Many companies invest heavily in recruitment but lose employees just as quickly due to weak onboarding. Without a structured, thoughtful onboarding process, even the best new hires can feel lost, disengaged, or unsure about their future. That's why onboarding sets the foundation for your team's long-term success. Let's explore how to create an onboarding experience that drives retention and engagement from day one.

When expectations are unclear, careers falter. When onboarding lacks direction, talent walks out the door—because it's easier than ever before to do so.

At this point, I've shown you how to drive Generational Excellence and how to view attracting talent in a new light. Once you've set the foundation and start bringing in strong talent through intentional methods, it's time to onboard and develop that talent to set them up for long-term success with your organization.

Over the years, through countless interviews with professionals across generations, one challenge has consistently risen to the surface: a lack of clarity. Whether it's new hires feeling lost during onboarding or experienced team members unsure of their growth path, the result is the same—missed opportunities, wasted time and resources, and frustrated employees.

Let's be clear: Onboarding and development are not optional. A well-structured onboarding process ensures new employees become productive faster, reducing the risk of costly turnover and wasted training efforts. If done right, onboarding isn't about making people feel comfortable—it's about accelerating performance and getting them contributing to the business as quickly as possible for your investment to feel well worth it. They are critical investments that set the stage for success, longevity, and mutual trust. Done right, they can transform your workforce and significantly reduce turnover. Done poorly, they're a fast track to lost talent.

In this chapter, we'll break down how to implement an effective onboarding and development strategy that works for all generations and levels in your workforce.

A Personal Perspective: When Onboarding Fails

At twenty-one years old, I thought I had everything figured out. I landed a job at a Fortune 500 company, moved to a new city, and envisioned myself climbing the corporate ladder. The interview process was thorough, and I felt confident I was set up for success.

Fast-forward ten months: I left the company, disillusioned and burnt out.

What went wrong? Well, it all started with misaligned expectations: The role I stepped into was vastly different from what I imagined. I thought I knew what I was getting myself into, but from the relationship with my boss to the watercooler conversations with fellow coworkers, everything was just different than what I envisioned. When we talk to early twentysomethings in their first jobs out of school, most of them share similar experiences, ranging from a lack of clarity surrounding what time they should come to work, benefits, culture, etc.

The second thing that went wrong was the generic onboarding plan I was thrust into. The program treated everyone the same, ignoring our varied backgrounds and skill sets. I was a communication studies and political science double major from a liberal arts school and had peers in the same program that were finance majors and had ten-plus years of work experience. Our onboarding was the same, but I'll ask you now that you are a pro on the Generational Advantage: Do you think this streamlined onboarding worked for anyone?

Looking back, it's clear to me that the trajectory of my first career could have been entirely different with the right onboarding support. A personalized plan that recognized my strengths, consistent communication from leadership, and a clear growth trajectory could have made all the difference. And yet, despite the struggles, I wouldn't change that experience. It forced me to ask hard questions, uncover patterns in workplace dynamics, and eventually embark on the journey that brought me here to write this book. What initially felt like a professional misstep became the spark for an incredible career of learning, teaching, and improving workplace experiences for others. Onboarding defines the trajectory of both careers and organizations. When done well, it sets employees up for success and strengthens the company's long-term stability.

Now, through our work with hundreds of organizations, we've identified five pillars that can transform onboarding and development into a driver of retention, engagement, and growth.

The Five Pillars of Effective Onboarding and Development

1. Onboarding: Slow Down to Go Fast
2. Identify Clear Growth Plans with Flexibility
3. Map Out a Trajectory and Communicate It Clearly
4. Empower and Develop Your Top Talent
5. Reverse Mentorship: A Two-Way Street

1. Onboarding: Slow Down to Go Fast
You've heard the saying, "Hire slow, fire fast." Well, the same applies to onboarding: "Onboard slow to retain top talent (fast)." Rushing the process costs you top talent. Trust me, we've experienced this firsthand as a team, so if you've ever found yourself in this position, we understand the challenges.

A strong onboarding process takes time. Our research consistently shows that the most effective onboarding programs span an average of three months. We don't mean your new employees can't work for three months, but they shouldn't be handed the keys after the first week on the job. While it's tempting to have new hires dive into work immediately, thoughtful pacing ensures a smoother transition and greater long-term success. Onboarding should also feel authentic, which means incorporating real stories from team members of all generations. Sharing their wins and challenges creates an honest, relatable experience for new hires, grounding them in the realities of your workplace culture. Remember the authenticity mentioned in the last chapter? It stems throughout the entire employee lifecycle.

And remember, one size doesn't fit all. Tailoring onboarding plans to fit everyone's role, background, and skill set makes all the difference. Whether it's a seasoned professional transitioning into a leadership role or an entry-level team member taking their first career steps, a customized approach sets them—and your organization—up for success.

Even within our small team, we've experienced firsthand the value of tailoring onboarding to set team members up for success. After all, we've brought them on board to make meaningful contributions, right? By customizing the process to align with the role, experience level, and comfort with technology, we've found that while this approach requires more time up front, it consistently pays off in the long run.

> **Case Study: Transforming Onboarding for Long-Term Success**
> We partnered with a national financial services organization that was experiencing high turnover rates among new hires, particularly within their first ninety days. Their existing onboarding process lasted just three weeks, leaving employees feeling overwhelmed, unsupported, and unclear about their roles and growth opportunities. After conducting a thorough analysis of their turnover data and employee feedback via our Generational Assessment, we identified key gaps in the onboarding process, like how new hires didn't fully understand how their roles fit into the larger organizational goals. Additionally, employees felt disconnected from their direct supervisors, with only one scheduled check-in during the onboarding period, not to mention critical training sessions were compressed to just ten days, leaving little time for skill building or team bonding.
>
> To address these issues, we worked closely with the organization to overhaul their onboarding framework, transforming it into a six-week program designed for long-term success. The new process began with setting clear weekly milestones to give new employees a sense of structure and progress. Development plans were tailored to align individual goals with team and organizational objectives, facilitating a stronger sense of purpose.
>
> Managers played a key role in the redesign, committing to weekly one-on-one check-ins with their new hires. These sessions provided

opportunities to address concerns, offer feedback, and build rapport. Training sessions, once hurried and dense, were extended and reimagined as interactive modules. Employees engaged in group activities, participated in mentorship programs, and gained hands-on experience that reinforced learning. To complete the experience, cultural integration became a cornerstone of the program. Through team-building exercises and storytelling, new hires gained a deeper understanding of the organization's values and vision.

The results were significant. Within a year, the organization saw retention rates for the first ninety days climb by 35 percent. Employee satisfaction during onboarding surged by 42 percent, as reflected in post-onboarding surveys. Productivity among new hires rose by 20 percent, with employees reporting increased confidence in their roles. These improvements also brought tangible financial benefits as the reduction in premature departures significantly lowered hiring costs.

This transformation highlights the importance of thoughtful onboarding in reducing early turnover, supporting productivity, and setting employees up for long-term success. When companies invest in their new hires from day one, the returns are significant—both in attitude and in measurable outcomes.

2. Identify Clear Growth Plans with Flexibility
Professionals of all generations share a common need for clarity and direction in their careers. Questions like "Where am I going?" and "How will I get there?" resonate universally across industries and age groups. A clear growth plan provides the answers—and does so with flexibility.

The best career pathways are thoughtfully mapped out with defined milestones, required skills, and key experiences that guide employees toward advancement. But flexibility should be built into these plans, allowing room for changes as employees' interests shift or as organizational needs evolve. Additionally, it's important to tie career progression to compensation, providing a transparent view of how advancement translates to financial rewards.

> Take Ethan, a twenty-nine-year-old head of customer engagement at an AI company, as an example. Reflecting on his career, he shared, "I've left four jobs before thirty because companies didn't give me a clear idea of where I was headed. Without direction, I'm kind of just left to question what my future looks like." His experience underscores a critical message: Without a dynamic plan that balances structure and adaptability, talented employees are more likely to leave in search of opportunities where they feel valued and supported.
>
> By offering employees clear, flexible growth paths, you're sending a powerful message: "We value you. We're investing in you. And we see your future with us." This sense of investment builds loyalty, engagement, and retention.

3. Map Out a Trajectory and Communicate It Clearly

Building a career trajectory for employees is a critical step, but ensuring that it's communicated clearly is what makes it effective. Transparency should begin during the interview process, where expectations are outlined, and continue through onboarding, where those expectations are reinforced. Regular check-ins, such as performance reviews or one-on-one meetings, are essential for aligning goals and addressing any concerns. These conversations must go both ways—creating space for employees to voice their aspirations, share feedback, and ask questions.

In my first role, my manager and I frequently found ourselves talking past each other. The intergenerational communication gaps we faced, combined with a lack of transparency, only deepened the disconnect. These types of communication breakdowns are common, but entirely avoidable with intentionality and structure. By prioritizing clarity and open dialogue, organizations can strengthen trust and ensure alignment between employee and employer expectations.

4. Empower and Develop Your Top Talent
Investing in professional development is no longer optional—it's a necessity. According to our 2023 GPS report, companies that prioritize professional development are 34 percent more likely to retain their employees. Development initiatives should encompass a range of opportunities, from providing access to workshops and training sessions to encouraging participation in conferences or mentorship programs. Employees feel empowered when given stretch opportunities—assignments or projects that challenge them to grow beyond their current roles. These initiatives should be personalized, aligning with each employee's unique strengths and career ambitions.

When employees feel that their organization is genuinely committed to their success, they feel valued—and that sense of value translates to stronger loyalty and retention. While investing in development is certainly a perk for your employees, it's more than that. It's a strategic approach to building a workforce that's engaged, motivated, and equipped for the future!

5. Reverse Mentorship: A Two-Way Street
While traditional mentorship models, where senior professionals guide younger employees, remain invaluable, reverse mentorship has emerged as a transformative approach. It creates a reciprocal dynamic where both parties contribute and gain. For example, a

younger professional might bring fresh perspectives on emerging technologies while a seasoned leader offers strategic guidance and deep industry knowledge.

Reverse mentorship bridges generations, driving innovation and strengthening intergenerational communication. By intentionally pairing employees from different age groups and investing in a structured mentorship plan, organizations can create relationships built on mutual trust and collaboration. Open, judgment-free conversations between mentors and mentees are key to unlocking the potential of this model.

If you're wondering how to get senior leaders on board with reverse mentorship, it might be worth revisiting the foundational steps of the Talent Impact Process. Leaders who embrace Generational Excellence are more likely to see reverse mentorship as a growth opportunity rather than a role reversal. With the right mindset, they'll be eager to learn from their younger counterparts while sharing their own wisdom in return.

> **KEY TAKEAWAYS FROM CHAPTER 6:**
>
> - A well-structured onboarding process is critical for retention, engagement, and long-term employee success. Rushing onboarding leads to overwhelmed employees and higher turnover.
> - Customizing onboarding plans to align with the diverse backgrounds and skill sets of employees creates stronger connections and trust.
> - Clear growth trajectories and flexible development paths empower employees of all generations to see their future within the organization.
> - Thoughtful onboarding reduces early turnover, increases productivity, and sets employees up for long-term success by aligning expectations and providing consistent communication.

Your Next Steps

If you're ready to invest in Onboarding and Development, here's where to begin:

1. **Identify Responsibility:** Determine who on your HR and development teams will own this initiative.
2. **Audit Your Current Process:** Evaluate what's working, where the gaps are, and how you can improve.
3. **Customize Plans:** Develop tailored onboarding and growth plans for entry-level, mid-level, and leadership roles.

4. **Implement a Mentorship Program:** Introduce formal two-way mentorship and track its impact.
5. **Communicate Clearly:** Set expectations early, map out trajectories, and maintain open communication.

> **PRO TIP:** Start simple. Team highlights videos, employee stories, and internal YouTube channels are effective, scalable tools that make onboarding engaging and personal.

> Dive deeper with your downloadable worksheet and apply what you've learned right away. Visit:
> https://thegenerationaladvantage.com/get-downloads/

Onboarding and development are investments in your employees' success and your organization's future. When done right, they improve clarity, trust, and loyalty, creating a workforce that grows with you, not away from you.

Up next in the GPS Talent Impact Process: Retention and Activation.

CHAPTER 7

RETENTION AND ACTIVATION: TURNING TALENT INTO LOYALTY

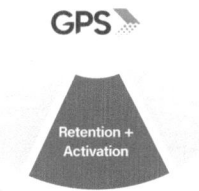

You're halfway through the GPS Talent Impact Process, and here's where the magic happens: keeping the talent you've worked so hard to attract, onboard, and develop.

Before we move on, though, let's revisit what you have learned so far. We started by setting the foundational steps to achieving the Generational Advantage: Generational Excellence, attracting talent, and onboarding and development. The first three parts of the process are critical to identify and practice before moving on to the latter half of the wheel. Without Generational Excellence, you can't drive a successful hiring and talent attraction practice, and without a strong hiring and talent attraction practice, your talent onboarding and development will be set up to fail before you even begin.

The last three chapters focused on the foundational elements of the Talent Impact Process that prepare and equip your organization to attract and retain a high-achieving workforce. The next three chapters will cover the execution and engagement of the process that will ensure lasting success for you and your organization. That leaves the final component of the process, data, which I'll share more on later.

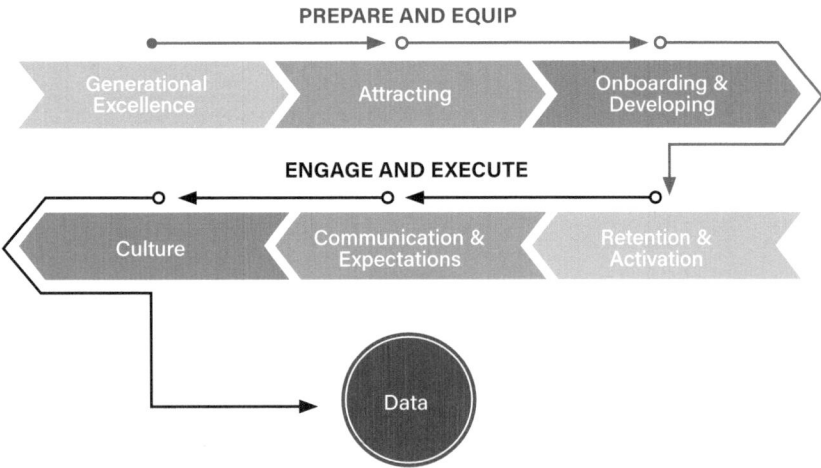

Now, let's begin with the fourth component of our process.

Retention goes beyond maintaining a payroll. It requires building an environment where employees across all generations feel engaged, motivated, and connected. Activation strengthens this by helping them reach their full potential and contribute meaningfully to the organization's success.

In this chapter, we'll dive into the four pillars of retention and activation:

1. Well-Being: The New Nonnegotiable
2. Compensation: More Than a Paycheck
3. Engagement: Connection Is Key
4. Digital Engagement: Use Technology to Retain Talent

RETENTION AND ACTIVATION: TURNING TALENT INTO LOYALTY

These areas work together to ensure your employees contribute to the long haul and grow with your organization—not out of it.

1. Well-Being: The New Nonnegotiable
Employee well-being—mental health, work-life balance, and holistic support—is no longer optional. The next generation of leaders grew up in a world where mental health was normalized and discussed. They bring this expectation into the workplace, but it does not have to be a bad thing.

For leaders who might think, *Well, we didn't have this. Why should they?*—times have changed. And here's why:

Data from a GPS's 2024 report shows that companies prioritizing mental health and well-being see higher retention rates and stronger performance outcomes. If you ignore this or intentionally dismiss it, you will miss out on top talent in years to come.

Creating a culture of well-being starts with tangible actions. Offering flexible sick days and mental health resources must be free from stigma, as encouraged days off don't work if employees fear judgment for using them. Employee Assistance Programs (EAPs) that provide counseling, financial guidance, and wellness workshops are becoming increasingly essential. Equally important are clear boundaries to prevent burnout—whether through defined work hours or optional "no meeting" days.

Take it from someone who has lived both sides of the equation. Throughout my career, I've experienced organizations that prioritized well-being and those that didn't. The difference couldn't have been clearer. In one role, where flexibility and a focus on mental and physical health were afterthoughts, I quickly realized it wasn't sustainable. I distinctly remember not getting up from my cubicle to get water or go to the bathroom for ten hours on countless occasions. In another, where well-being was not just acknowledged but actively supported, I was thriving. The flexibility, attention to mental health, and commitment to holistic wellness left me more fulfilled and, in turn, more productive in my role.

> **Case Study: How Wellness Wednesdays Boosted Team Health**
> One of the best examples I've seen comes from a midsize tech firm for which we led a workshop. During a session, they developed and launched an employee-led "Wellness Wednesday" initiative. This included short monthly workshops on stress management, mindfulness, and physical wellness, tailored to meet the needs of their multigenerational team. Each week, a volunteer brought a healthy snack of the day and encouraged lunchtime walks. The results spoke for themselves: a 16 percent drop in absenteeism and a noticeable improvement in team culture.

When organizations prioritize employee well-being, the benefits go beyond engagement and retention. A culture that genuinely supports its people creates a workplace where employees take pride in their contributions.

Well-being is not an extra benefit—it's a strategic approach to keeping employees committed and motivated.

2. Compensation: More Than a Paycheck
As Jason Richards, a guest on our podcast *The Great Retention*, said, "Too many people rely on compensation alone. If someone's making a lot of money but isn't fulfilled, they're going to leave."

Compensation *has* evolved. For young professionals, salary and financial stability are now top priorities—thanks to rising costs, student loan debt, and economic uncertainty. This has not always been the case in our research. In our first survey back in 2018, we learned that compensation was ranked significantly lower than other factors, including communication (#1), meaningful work (#2), and culture (#3).

While competitive pay helps attract talent, it alone isn't enough to keep them. If compensation isn't paired with growth opportunities, culture, and engagement, retention will suffer.

How to Build a Compensation Strategy That Retains Talent

Building an effective compensation strategy starts with understanding the market. Conducting thorough research to benchmark salaries against industry standards ensures your offerings remain competitive. But a competitive salary isn't enough; structure and transparency are equally important. Employees want to understand how salaries, bonuses, and benefits are structured and why. Clear communication about these factors goes a long way in building trust and loyalty.

A strong compensation strategy also includes regular reviews. Salaries and bonus opportunities should be updated to reflect market trends, employee performance, and company growth. Balancing internal equity is another critical component—particularly when hiring new talent. While high starting salaries can attract strong candidates, they must be carefully balanced to avoid alienating experienced employees who may feel undervalued by comparison. I can't tell you how many times our team has seen this in recent years. Without thoughtful alignment, resentment and turnover could undermine even the best-intentioned hiring decisions.

We understand that creating a compensation strategy can feel daunting, which is why we frequently collaborate with compensation specialists who bring expertise and actionable insights to the table. These professionals can help you fine-tune your approach and ensure it aligns with industry trends and employee expectations.

If this feels overwhelming, start small. Begin with an internal audit of your current compensation structure. Ask yourself: How can we be competitive, fair, and prepare for the future? Small incremental changes can have a big impact on retaining top talent and advancing a positive culture.

3. Engagement: Connection Is Key
Engagement goes beyond keeping employees happy. It's about creating a workplace where employees feel connected, motivated, and valued. When employees see purpose in their work and feel a part of something larger than themselves, the results are transformative. GPS's research consistently shows that engaged employees are far more likely to remain with their organizations, with 87 percent reporting stronger commitment and greater satisfaction. They also contribute to a more positive workplace culture, creating ripple effects across teams.

> **Case Study: How One Firm Turned a Milestone into Momentum**
> The importance of engagement came to life during our work with an engineering firm celebrating its tenth anniversary. Together, we developed a comprehensive employee engagement strategy to mark the milestone. The initiative included recognition programs (including on their social media channels!) to celebrate individual and team achievements, a family-friendly team retreat complete with an awards ceremony, and long-term engagement initiatives designed to sustain the momentum long after the anniversary celebrations ended. The result? Employees not only felt appreciated but also deeply connected to the company's mission and future, which had lasting impacts on its productivity and bottom line.

This case highlights the importance of sustained engagement. One-off initiatives might generate short-term enthusiasm, but lasting impact comes from consistently reinforcing purpose, strengthening connections, and ensuring employees feel valued in their daily work.

True engagement is woven into everyday interactions and organizational culture—not something checked off a list.

4. Digital Engagement: Use Technology to Retain Talent

Your digital platforms can do more than attract talent—they're vital for keeping employees engaged and connected, especially with younger generations who are digital natives. These tools allow organizations to celebrate success, share stories, and cultivate meaningful connections in a format that feels natural to today's workforce.

One effective way to leverage digital tools is by highlighting team achievements and milestones. Social media and internal platforms provide an opportunity to recognize certifications, accomplishments, and even day-to-day wins. For instance, creating authentic content such as "Day in the Life" videos or "Meet the Team" spotlights can showcase your company culture in a way that feels genuine and relatable. We do this on our own GPS channels, so take a look for some inspiration if you're feeling lost. I'll also note that whenever we promote our team online, there's always extra pep in their step. It does not take much to recognize your team, so consider making it a priority as part of your overall retention strategy.

Digital platforms can also build connection by offering professional development resources, fostering employee groups, or running quick polls to gather feedback. These actions signal that you're not just listening to your team but actively investing in their growth and satisfaction. In a workplace increasingly shaped by technology, leveraging these tools effectively can help ensure that employees feel valued, seen, and engaged, which, again, will only increase productivity and results.

Recognition doesn't have to be public to be powerful. While social media can be a great tool, it's not the only—or always the best—way to celebrate your team. Some employees prefer a shoutout in a team meeting, a note in an internal newsletter, or even a simple handwritten message that acknowledges their contributions. Understanding how each person prefers to be recognized isn't just thoughtful—it's strategic. It builds trust, boosts retention, and can save you time and resources in the long run.

Case Study: Why One Plastics Manufacturer Stopped Hiding Its Best People
When we first partnered with a midsize manufacturer in the Midwest, their leadership expressed a major concern: They hesitated to highlight employees on social media. Their fear? Showcasing their team's skills and achievements might make them easy targets for competitors or recruiters looking to poach top talent. After analyzing their employee engagement data through our Generational Assessment, we discovered an even bigger issue—team members felt underappreciated and disconnected from the company's leadership. The employer's reluctance to celebrate their employees was inadvertently signaling that their contributions weren't valued.

Our advice was simple: If your organization implements the GPS Talent Impact Process, retaining talent becomes less about hiding them and more about building loyalty through recognition. The team decided to take a leap of faith.

They began regularly posting about employee milestones, such as industry certifications, completed projects, and community involvement. For example, when a senior team member achieved a prestigious certification, they highlighted his journey in a LinkedIn post, reaching over twelve thousand views! And during their annual company meeting, they showcased the volunteer efforts of their entire team, sparking positive engagement from both employees and clients.

RETENTION AND ACTIVATION: TURNING TALENT INTO LOYALTY

> Employee morale improved by 30 percent within six months, as measured by an internal engagement survey. The organization saw a 22 percent increase in retention rates over the following year, with employees frequently citing recognition as a key motivator. Social media engagement grew by 45 percent, helping attract new candidates who resonated with the organization's culture.
>
> Recognition boosts engagement, but it ripples beyond that. Recognition is a long-term investment in loyalty and a culture where employees feel valued and motivated to contribute more. By celebrating their people publicly, the organization turned a perceived risk into one of their most effective tools for retention and recruitment.

This chapter explored the dual components of retention and activation—both essential for maximizing your workforce's potential. Retaining top talent is only half the equation, though. The real impact comes when you activate that talent. Activation means inspiring your team to go beyond their roles, becoming ambassadors for your organization both within and outside the workplace. It's about creating a culture where employees naturally champion your business, attract new talent and clients, and represent your brand with pride. When you activate talent, you not only set them up for success—you maximize their performance. At this point in the book, I don't really need to tell you this because you already know that when employees feel engaged and valued, their enthusiasm becomes contagious, creating a ripple effect that strengthens your organization's reputation, builds loyalty, and drives sustainable success. And who doesn't want that?

> **KEY TAKEAWAYS FROM CHAPTER 7:**
>
> - Well-being has become a critical retention strategy. Prioritizing mental health, work-life balance, and holistic employee support leads to higher retention rates and stronger performance.
> - Compensation strategies must go beyond competitive salaries. Transparency, equity, and alignment with growth opportunities ensure long-term loyalty, satisfaction, and productivity.
> - Engagement drives retention. Employees who feel connected to their work and the organization are 87 percent more likely to stay, making intentional engagement practices a cornerstone of success.
> - Digital engagement tools—such as social media recognition, employee storytelling, and online learning resources—offer modern, effective ways to retain and activate talent, especially among younger, tech-savvy generations.

Your Next Steps

Retention and activation require a multifaceted approach. In order to see results here, your team needs to feel:

- Supported through well-being programs that show you care about them as people.
- Rewarded with competitive, transparent compensation strategies.
- Connected through consistent engagement and recognition.
- Valued with tools, opportunities, and development that meet them where they are.

RETENTION AND ACTIVATION: TURNING TALENT INTO LOYALTY

Below are the action steps to begin retaining and activating your team today:

1. **Complete an audit** of your current mental health and well-being offerings.
2. **Create a wish list** of high-yield programs to implement this year.
3. **Conduct a market analysis** to ensure you're offering competitive salaries.
4. **Complete an audit of your compensation strategy** and determine a plan to communicate it.
5. Design or refresh your **Employee Engagement Program**.
6. **Start simple:** Try posting "**meet the team**" features or survey your team for recognition preferences.

> Dive deeper with your downloadable worksheet and apply what you've learned right away. Visit:
> https://thegenerationaladvantage.com/get-downloads/

Retention isn't about trying to hold employees hostage with high salaries and "golden handcuffs." It's about creating an environment where they *want* to stay, grow, and contribute. When your team feels valued, supported, and recognized, they won't just stay—they'll flourish—and your organization will thrive.

Up next in the GPS Talent Impact Process: Step 5—Communication and Expectations. This is where we bridge gaps, align goals, and set the foundation for long-term success.

CHAPTER 8

COMMUNICATION AND EXPECTATIONS: CREATING CONNECTION

Nine times out of ten, when there's a workplace challenge, it all boils down to communication.

As I've traveled across the country and internationally to speak on this topic, countless leaders have approached me with a familiar question: "What makes your solutions any different? Communication has always been an issue—and it always will be." It's a fair question, and after hearing it enough times, I've made a point to address it head-on at the start of my sessions about intergenerational communication. So I'll do the same here.

Here's the truth: They're absolutely right. Communication challenges have existed for decades—likely centuries—and they aren't going to disappear overnight. However, the workplace has never been better positioned to address these issues than it is today. With more generational knowledge at our fingertips and a deeper understanding of intergenerational dynamics, we now have a unique opportunity to reshape how we communicate, not just across generations, but with individuals.

Miscommunication creates false assumptions. Poorly set expectations lead to frustration, inefficiency, and turnover. No matter how strong your efforts have been in Generational Excellence, attraction, onboarding and development, or retention, they will fall apart without effective communication and clear expectations.

Think of communication and expectations as the connectors—the activators that bring the first four steps of the Talent Impact Process to life and pave the way for culture and data, the final steps in the GPS Talent Impact Process.

Let's break it down into three key focus areas:

1. Communication Preferences and Styles
2. Communication Tools
3. Setting Expectations Clearly

1. Communication Preferences and Styles
Every person has a preferred way of communicating, and when these preferences are ignored, problems arise. Whether it's a preference for face-to-face conversations, emails, instant messaging, or phone calls, understanding these styles is critical.

Consider the variation in communication styles across generations. While baby boomers often lean toward direct interactions like meetings or phone calls, Gen Xers may prefer balancing between emails and video conferencing. Millennials gravitate to platforms such as Slack or Teams for instant communication, whereas Gen Zers, while adept with collaborative tools, also value face-to-face engagement—on their own terms.

COMMUNICATION AND EXPECTATIONS: CREATING CONNECTION

Case Study: It's Not What You Say, It's How You Say It
A recent situation we encountered in local government highlights the impact of these differences. A baby boomer city planner expected a critical report as a printed copy on their desk, but the Gen Z associate, accustomed to digital workflows, submitted it via email. With no prior discussion on expectations, frustration brewed, leading to HR intervention and the eventual resignation of the associate.

This case illustrates that communication missteps often stem not from content but from delivery. The simplest solution is to just ask! During onboarding or team meetings, open a dialogue about preferred communication styles. Acknowledging and sharing these preferences ignites mutual respect and lays the groundwork for a more cohesive and effective team dynamic. It's also a crucial step in the process to acknowledge your own communication styles as a leader. How else can you expect your team to adapt, respond effectively, or feel confident in how they communicate with you?

By prioritizing these conversations, you minimize misunderstandings, streamline workflows, and cultivate a team culture built on respect and clarity. For example, I keep our team's communication preferences chart in my notebook at all times. It's my go-to reminder of how to reach each team member in the way that works best for them—whether it's for routine updates or critical needs. I know our graphic designer, for instance, doesn't check emails often while deep in design work and tends to be most productive late at night or early in the morning. When I wake up, I often see her notes waiting for me. Similarly, our associate consultant responds quickly to texts, works early in the morning, and picks back up in the afternoon after family time. While I don't communicate with them according to their preferred methods daily, the key is that I understand how they work best. In return, they understand how I communicate best, too, and as leaders, it's important for you to communicate this to your team as well. This mutual understanding allows us to create a flexible work environment where everyone thrives and motivates our team in new ways in the process.

Since hiring our first employees in 2022, we've celebrated countless team anniversaries, and I look forward to recognizing many more milestones in the future. These anniversaries are a testament to the power of communication, adaptability, and trust in building a team that stays committed and engaged. That said, I know there are business owners reading this who are growing their teams and thinking, *"It's not always this smooth."* And you're right—it isn't. We're fortunate to have such incredible team members who've joined us on this wild journey, but communication, as rewarding as it is, can often be messy and complex. That's why tools like our communication preferences chart go straight back to the basics—and really make such a difference. They bring structure and clarity to something that is inherently nuanced, helping to advance better collaboration and understanding across the board.

I would encourage you to try recreating this for your own team—it usually stirs up some great conversation, and you can download a tool like this at the end of the chapter.

Name	Preferred	Urgent
Employee #1	Email	Text
Employee #2	In Person	Phone Call
Employee #3	Text	Phone Call

COMMUNICATION AND EXPECTATIONS: CREATING CONNECTION

Name	Preferred	Urgent
Employee #4	Phone Call	Email
Employee #5	Email	Text
Employee #6	Slack	In Person
Employee #7	Slack	Text

2. Communication Tools: Meeting the Needs of Every Generation
The right tools make communication seamless. The wrong ones cause chaos.

In multigenerational workplaces, the tools you choose should balance familiarity (for experienced professionals) and innovation (for younger professionals).

The tools we use shape how we connect. For younger generations, Slack might feel like an extension of thought; for more experienced professionals, email provides clarity and formality. Neither is wrong—it's about finding the right tool for the right moment.

> **Case Study: Finding the Right Channel—Modernizing Communication Without Losing Your Team**
> Consider a marketing team that implemented Slack (an internal communication tool) channels for project updates. At first, the baby boomers on the team resisted, favoring email threads instead. But once they were guided through Slack's functionality and how it saves time for quick updates, people picked up on it. Instead of replacing emails, the team used Slack for brainstorming and real-time collaboration, reserving email for formal communications.

Reality Check: Not every baby boomer struggles with technology. In fact, this narrative often feels outdated and misleading. At nearly every speaking event I attend, at least one baby boomer enthusiastically shares, "I text more than half my twenty-five-year-old coworkers!" It's a reminder that assumptions about generational tech habits don't always hold up and that adaptability spans all ages.

The Right Tool for the Right Moment

Here's an example of settings where these channels make the most sense across clients we have worked with.

1. Email: For detailed updates, formal communication, and documentation
2. Instant Messaging: For quick questions and informal updates (Slack/Teams)
3. Video Conferencing: For face-to-face collaboration and clarity in remote settings
4. Social Media: For engagement, recognition, and team storytelling
5. Project Management Tools: For tracking progress and assigning accountability

> **PRO TIP**: Introduce new tools thoughtfully. Provide training sessions to ensure everyone—regardless of generation—feels confident using them.

COMMUNICATION AND EXPECTATIONS: CREATING CONNECTION

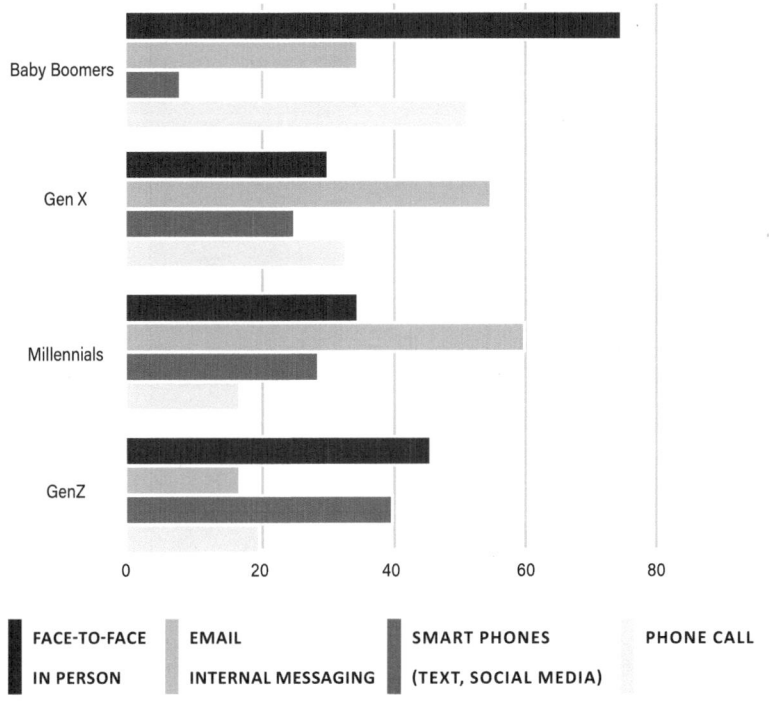

COMMUNICATION TOOLS—PREFERENCES ACROSS GENERATIONS
SOURCE: Generational Performance Solutions (2025)

3. Setting Expectations Clearly
Effective communication is built on clear expectations. Without guidelines for how, when, and why tools are used, miscommunication can derail even the best teams. I have found that this is where many leaders struggle—leaving too much gray area around communication norms, which leads to confusion, inefficiency, and frustration on all sides.

Case Study: Too Many Tools, Not Enough Clarity
One hospitality group experienced this firsthand when they introduced multiple communication platforms—email, a property management system (PMS) messaging tool, and a scheduling app—but failed to establish clear boundaries. Employees weren't sure which tool to use for which purpose. Guest requests were buried in email chains, shift changes were discussed on the wrong platform, and critical updates were overlooked. The result was confusion, delayed responses, and unnecessary frustration across teams.

A clear communication guidelines document, like the one you see below, that outlined the role of each tool and set expectations for their use. For example, email was reserved for company-wide updates or policy changes, the PMS messaging tool was designated for real-time guest service issues, and the scheduling app became the single source of truth for shift changes. By defining when and why each tool should be used, teams gained clarity, reduced inefficiencies, and improved response times—leading to better service and a smoother operation. We have seen success from this across many industries, not just hospitality.

TEAM COMMUNICATION GUIDELINES
Team members must be reachable on Slack and email between 9:00 AM and 5:00 PM EST, Monday–Friday. Any deviation (PTO, appointments) must be approved and noted on the shared calendar at least 2 weeks in advance.
Notify your manager and the project channel on Slack immediately if you are unable to attend a meeting or come to work. Text only if it's within 1 hour of the start time.
Schedule and complete 3 project-specific check-ins per week: 2 via Slack threads, and 1 via a 15-minute video call (Zoom or Teams). Track notes in the shared project doc.

COMMUNICATION AND EXPECTATIONS: CREATING CONNECTION

TEAM COMMUNICATION GUIDELINES
Submit next week's in-office/remote schedule by 2:00 PM Friday in the "#team-schedule" Slack channel. Update your Google Calendar accordingly.
For urgent issues, speak in-person or text (do not email). Confirm your team's preferred method for emergencies quarterly and document it in the team directory.

Establishing clear communication expectations also means defining boundaries. Set clear parameters, such as using email for updates that need to be referenced later, Slack or Teams for immediate but nonurgent needs, and phone or text for emergencies. This approach not only minimizes confusion but also builds trust within your team.

Creating a living communication guidelines document goes further. This playbook can outline preferred tools for different tasks, response time expectations, and emergency protocols. For instance, employees might respond to Slack messages within an hour, while emails are expected within twenty-four hours. The document is living for a reason: Regularly updating this document ensures it stays relevant as communication needs evolve. With our digital resource library, you now have access to your own customizable communication guidelines template. I encourage you to take the time to complete it—write out what's expected, when, and how. If you're assuming your team just "gets it," that's your cue to document it. Clear expectations eliminate confusion, save time, and build trust. Put it in writing. Share it with your team. You'll be glad you did.

By setting clear expectations, you build transparency, accountability, and trust. No one's left guessing—or frustrated—about when or how to communicate.

Communication and expectations bring the GPS Talent Impact Process to life. When you acknowledge communication preferences, choose the right tools, and set clear guidelines, you create an environment of trust, clarity, and efficiency.

> **KEY TAKEAWAYS FROM CHAPTER 8:**
>
> - Tailoring communication tools to team needs, from instant messaging to face-to-face meetings, helps bridge generational gaps and create seamless collaboration.
> - Setting clear communication guidelines, such as when and how to use specific tools, promotes accountability and ensures clarity across all levels of the organization.
> - Acknowledging and aligning communication preferences and tools enhances productivity, reduces frustration, and builds trust in a multigenerational workforce.

 **Your Next Steps**

1. **Assess:** Review your team's current communication practices. What's working? What's not?
2. **Ask:** Identify each team member's communication preferences.
3. **Choose Tools:** Select tools that align with your team's needs and provide training to ensure everyone is proficient.
4. **Set Expectations:** Create and share a communication guidelines document.
5. **Review:** Regularly revisit and adjust your strategies to ensure ongoing effectiveness.

COMMUNICATION AND EXPECTATIONS: CREATING CONNECTION

> Dive deeper with your downloadable worksheet and apply what you've learned right away. Visit:
> https://thegenerationaladvantage.com/get-downloads/

Clear, effective communication transforms teams and further enhances the Generational Advantage. It removes ambiguity, reduces frustration, and builds stronger relationships. By aligning communication preferences, tools, and expectations, you'll unlock a workplace where employees—from all generations—are connected, engaged, and productive.

Up Next: Step 6—Culture. This is where everything you've implemented so far comes together to build an environment that people are proud to be part of. Let's dive into it.

CHAPTER 9

CULTURE: THE FOUNDATION FOR MULTIGENERATIONAL SUCCESS

At this point in the Talent Impact Process, we just have two remaining components of the wheel left to explore. How are you feeling?

My hope is that you've started to see how the Generational Advantage can work alongside your organization and help you see long-term success for years to come. The coolest part about this process? It works in tandem with your HR and operations teams and can align with your goals, so it's not impeding progress but rather enhancing it.

Now let's talk about culture, the penultimate step in our book. It's one of the most overused buzzwords in business today, yet it remains one of the most misunderstood concepts. To be clear, I don't claim to have all the answers when it comes to culture. There are countless brilliant experts in this space, including a few dear friends of mine, who dedicate their work to this topic. Where we focus our expertise is on culture as it relates to a multigenerational workforce. If you're searching for resources on culture more broadly, I highly recommend exploring the wealth of incredible books, tools, and organizations devoted to the subject. A few of my favorites include *Unreasonable Hospitality* by Will Guidara, *Culture Shock* by Jim Clifton and Jim Harter of Gallup, and *Radical Candor* by Kim Scott—just to name a few.

So what is culture, really?

For the purposes of the GPS Talent Impact Process, we define culture as:

> The collective personality of your organization, driven by its values, behaviors, beliefs, and actions shared among employees.

In short, it's how you *show up* as an organization and how that experience makes people feel, driving their motivation and performance.

I can already hear some leaders groaning at the phrase "how that experience makes people feel."

But let me ask you this: If you had a proven tool to maximize profitability, purpose, and performance, wouldn't you use it?

That's precisely the potential of a culture rooted in strong, authentic values, supported by aligned behaviors, beliefs, and actions across your team. I'm going to show you how you do that in this chapter.

After interviewing thousands of young professionals and experienced leaders over the past seven years, one thing stands out: Culture directly determines retention, engagement, and performance.

A 2024 Deloitte report found that while 93 percent of executives and 88 percent of employees agree that companies should create value for both shareholders and society, workplace culture remains a challenge.[11] The same Deloitte study revealed that 60 percent of employees have engaged in "covering" behaviors—downplaying aspects of their identity to fit in—highlighting persistent gaps between stated company values and employees' lived experiences.

CULTURE: THE FOUNDATION FOR MULTIGENERATIONAL SUCCESS

Why does this matter? Because no amount of money will make someone stay in a poor culture. Trust us, we've seen it over and over again. In this chapter, we'll explore how to build a culture that drives performance and profitability, strengthens credibility, and enhances productivity.

We'll focus on four pillars of a strong culture:

1. Values: The Foundation of Culture
2. Behaviors: Values in Action
3. Beliefs: Shaping Your Organization's Mindset
4. Actions: Culture in Motion

Let's break it down.

1. Values: The Foundation of Culture
Values are the backbone of your organization. They define what you stand for and guide decision-making at every level. But here's the challenge: Values can't just live on your website or office walls—they must be lived every day.

> **Case Study: Putting Their People Front and Center**
> A construction services client of ours in Greenville, South Carolina, lives and breathes their value of family and community. When I walked into their office for the first time, I was struck by their People Wall—a series of headshots celebrating every team member. What started as a small wall has now expanded to two, and it's moving with them to their larger headquarters this year.
>
> Why does this matter? Because they've built a culture where people genuinely feel valued and connected. Their wall serves as a daily reminder of that commitment—celebrating the individuals who shape the organization and reinforcing a sense of belonging.

> **PRO TIP**: Ask yourself, "Are our values visible, meaningful, and lived out?" If not, start small. Highlight stories, people, or programs that embody your values.

Another layer of this foundation is a culture of feedback, which can be formed through a generationally inclusive culture. Does your organization have a culture where all generations feel comfortable giving feedback? If you don't know how to answer that question, it's likely an area of growth for your team, and that is okay!

> **Case Study: How One Manufacturer Boosted Engagement from the Ground Up**
> During a generational assessment we conducted with a manufacturing client, the leadership team identified consistent, open feedback as a critical driver of success. As part of the initiative, the company installed anonymous feedback boxes on the shop floor and in break rooms—making it easy for employees at all levels to share

ideas, concerns, and suggestions. What set this effort apart was the follow-through: The leaders acted on the feedback they received. One employee suggestion led to revamped shift communication protocols; another sparked the launch of a peer recognition program to celebrate individual milestones publicly. By showing that input was not only welcomed but implemented, the company empowered employees to take ownership and feel genuinely valued. The result? Stronger communication, increased engagement, and a culture grounded in growth, inclusion, and shared success.

2. Behaviors: Values in Action

Values are meaningless without behaviors that back them up. The way employees at all levels act and interact determines whether your culture aligns with your stated values.

Imagine a company that touts work-life balance as a core value. Yet leaders send emails at 10:00 p.m., praise employees for working late, and frown upon taking PTO. Do you see the disconnect? When behaviors contradict values, culture suffers. Employees lose trust, engagement declines, and retention becomes a challenge.

Work environments play a huge role in shaping behaviors. Are your spaces—physical or virtual—designed to drive productivity, creativity, and collaboration? If not, this may be holding your team back.

A client in healthcare that we work with faced challenges in cultivating collaboration between faculty, students, and administrative staff, teams whose combined efforts were essential to advancing their mission of cutting-edge medical education and research. However, their office setup, dominated by private offices and long hallways, hindered interaction and teamwork.

By recommending via our generational assessment that they redesign their space to include shared lounges, breakout rooms, and centralized collaborative areas, we helped create an environment that encouraged spontaneous conversations and cross-generational brainstorming. Within six months, they saw a significant 12 percent increase in team collaboration metrics, resulting in more innovative research proposals and smoother administrative processes.

Consider evaluating whether your team's behaviors align with your values and make necessary changes to your environment or leadership practices.

3. Beliefs: Shaping Your Organization's Mindset

Values and behaviors are critical, but they only take root when your team *believes* in them.

A strong culture ensures that every employee—regardless of their background, role, or tenure—feels seen, heard, and valued. A workplace culture that creates belonging allows employees to bring their full selves to work, creating an environment where collaboration, innovation, and trust can grow. When employees feel they are valued as individuals, their engagement and commitment increase, and the organization benefits. In fact, inclusive environments consistently outperform those that fail to prioritize a sense of belonging.

Flexibility has become a hallmark of successful workplace cultures. Hybrid work models, remote options, and adaptable schedules offer employees the autonomy to balance their personal and professional lives.

> **Case Study: How Supporting Caregivers Boosted Productivity by 17%**
>
> For instance, a global marketing firm realized how caregiving responsibilities were affecting the productivity of senior employees. One creative director struggled to meet deadlines while caring for her aging parents within the constraints of rigid office hours. By implementing flexible schedules and hybrid work options, the firm

> empowered this employee and others to balance their personal and professional responsibilities effectively without diminishing their contributions. The result? A 17 percent increase in team productivity and a noticeable boost in attitude across their team.

It's worth emphasizing here that flexibility isn't only a preference of younger workers—it's a universal need. While remote work and hybrid options are often associated with Gen Z or the youngest employees, employees across all age groups value flexibility. Life stages, caregiving responsibilities, and individual circumstances play a significant role in shaping what flexibility means to each person. Recognizing and addressing these needs not only builds trust but also strengthens engagement and performance organization-wide.

When workplace policies reflect employees' needs, organizations see higher retention, stronger engagement, and a more committed workforce.

Flexibility plays a critical role in employee performance, giving them autonomy to balance responsibilities and stay engaged in their work.

4. Actions: Culture in Motion

Culture comes to life through intentional action. It's what your team *does* every day to support your values, behaviors, and beliefs.

Engagement is one of the strongest indicators of a healthy workplace culture. Are your employees actively contributing to the organization's success? Do they feel heard, respected, and valued? In Chapter 7, we explored how to retain and activate talent through meaningful engagement strategies, including the engineering firm's tenth anniversary initiative. That example demonstrated the power of engagement during a specific event; now, let's take that concept further by embedding it into the organization's everyday culture.

THE GENERATIONAL ADVANTAGE

Case Study: How One Engineering Firm Turned Values into Engagement

Another engineering firm, with just over forty employees, exemplifies what it means to bring culture to life. Their values—team-focused, foresight and planning, and personal commitment—are spotlighted on a corkboard right as you walk into their office. However, these values are more than words on a wall. They influence how employees show up and engage daily.

We collaborated with the firm to create a social media strategy centered around their people, celebrating milestones and highlighting achievements that stemmed from those initial words and values. The pride within their team was palpable. Employees eagerly reshared posts, celebrated each other's successes, and became ambassadors for the company's culture.

The impact was undeniable: improved recruitment efforts, stronger retention, and a thriving workplace where employees felt genuinely connected to the organization's mission.

CULTURE: THE FOUNDATION FOR MULTIGENERATIONAL SUCCESS

Culture isn't really a buzzword at all—it's the heartbeat of your organization if properly launched. It determines whether your employees stay, make an impact, or leave. By focusing on values, behaviors, beliefs, and actions, you'll build a culture that fuels engagement, productivity, and retention.

KEY TAKEAWAYS FROM CHAPTER 9:

- Culture is the collective personality of your organization, shaped by its values, behaviors, beliefs, and actions.

- Aligning workplace environments with your culture, whether physical or virtual, fosters collaboration, innovation, and team cohesion.

- Inclusion and flexibility are essential beliefs that shape a thriving culture, ensuring every generation feels valued and empowered to contribute.

- Culture comes to life through intentional actions, such as celebrating milestones, prioritizing engagement, and aligning policies with employee needs.

- Organizations with strong, authentic cultures attract top talent, retain employees, and achieve greater long-term success.

 **Your Next Steps**

If you're ready to build a culture that drives performance, here's where to begin:

1. **Audit Your Current Culture:** Evaluate your values, behaviors, and beliefs. Are they aligned?
2. **Make Values Visible and Actionable:** Incorporate your values into performance reviews, onboarding, and recognition programs.
3. **Prioritize Engagement:** Launch initiatives that involve employees at all levels. Consider surveys, town halls, and team-building activities. Ensure cross-generational voices are included in decision-making.
4. **Embrace Flexibility:** Assess your policies around hybrid work, PTO, and schedules.
5. **Showcase Your Culture:** Start small with visible initiatives like a People Wall or team recognition posts.

Remember: culture is what you do, not what you say. Live it, and your team will too.

> Dive deeper with your downloadable worksheet and apply what you've learned right away. Visit:
> https://thegenerationaladvantage.com/get-downloads/

Up Next: The final step of the GPS Talent Impact Process—Data. Get ready to align your culture with forward-thinking practices that ensure long-term success.

CHAPTER 10

DATA-DRIVEN DECISIONS: THE GENERATIONAL PLAYBOOK

Well, you've made it. If you're still with me, congratulations. You're clearly committed to building a stronger, more generationally conscious workplace. We've explored the execution and engagement portions of the Talent Impact Process, which means there's just one crucial step left to tackle: Data. Let's dive in.

This brings everything we've covered over the last nine chapters home. It is also the most future-oriented part of the Talent Impact Process and has everything to do with the longevity of your organization and the kind of impact you want to make as a leader, if not now, then one day soon.

Data doesn't just tell us where we are—it shows us where we're going.

When I first started YoPro Know, now Generational Performance Solutions, I built the foundation on data, specifically insights from young professionals (YoPros). This data gave us a front-row seat to understanding their challenges, motivations, and behaviors, and it became a tool for companies to attract, retain, and engage top talent. Of course, as you now know, this evolved into collecting stories and facts about their counterparts: experienced professionals. What are their challenges, motivations, behaviors, etc.?

But the real power of data isn't just about understanding today's workforce. It's about using that knowledge to prepare for the future.

What will the rise of AI mean for your team's roles? How will Generation Alpha—and soon after, Generation Beta—change the way we work, hire, and lead?

The organizations that use data proactively will not only stay ahead but will also bear their anchor in this fast-changing landscape.

In this chapter, we'll explore two major areas:

1. Leveraging Generational Data
2. Preparing for Future Generations

1. Leveraging Generational Data
Generational data allows you to make strategic, informed decisions that drive results. We can no longer just understand preferences—it's all about acting on them now.

Consider this: Our data shows that Gen Z candidates are significantly more likely to respond to a text invitation for an interview than an email. So why are organizations still relying on outdated email-only approaches, waiting days for responses? Recruiters who adopted text-based outreach years ago saw a noticeable rise in interview attendance, simply by adapting their methods to meet candidates where they are.

Critics might argue that this approach could waste time by engaging candidates who might otherwise be filtered out. However, the reality is that these small data-driven adjustments often lead to higher engagement and better hiring outcomes. The goal is not to add more work but to make work more efficient by using tools and methods that align with today's workforce.

How Organizations Can Collect and Use Data

Understanding your workforce begins with asking the right questions and acting on the answers. In today's workplace, data is the key to unlocking your organization's full potential. By gathering meaningful insights into employee experiences, organizations can pinpoint challenges and uncover opportunities for growth.

> **Case Study: Data-Driven Retention—How a Law Firm Reduced Turnover by 40%**
> One of our clients, a law firm, faced challenges in retaining first-year associates. After reviewing engagement survey data, they pinpointed two major issues: unclear growth paths and the absence of effective mentorship. By implementing a structured onboarding process paired with a robust mentorship program, the firm achieved a 40 percent improvement in retention rates within just one year.

This example highlights how leveraging data can transform both talent acquisition and retention strategies. For instance, tracking metrics like time-to-hire, cost-per-hire, and quality of hires allows organizations to refine their recruitment processes based on clear evidence of what works. Similarly, analyzing retention data can uncover the underlying reasons employees leave—whether it's dissatisfaction with career development opportunities, compensation misalignments, or cultural disconnects. Once these trends are identified, targeted solutions can be developed to address them directly.

Case Study: Gen Z to the Polls—How Data Helped Drive Voter Engagement
Another example of a client using generational insights to drive measurable change comes from a recent project with a local initiative in South Carolina focused on voter engagement. Historically, voter participation among young professionals between the ages of twenty-one and thirty-nine had been low, particularly in primary elections. To address this challenge, the organization partnered with our team to conduct a generational assessment that examined how this age group received voting information, where they learned about candidates, and the barriers preventing them from registering and participating.

Our research revealed several key findings. Young professionals were significantly more likely to engage with visually compelling, short-form content on platforms such as Instagram and YouTube rather than long-form articles or traditional mailers. Sounds obvious, right? Yet many organizations and campaigns were relying on these tactics, not truly thinking about how different generations receive information in unique ways. Additionally, trust in information sources varied across the age spectrum, with younger millennials relying more on social media-driven news while older professionals in this group turned to official election websites. Many eligible voters also found the registration process unclear or inaccessible, often citing confusion around deadlines and requirements as a deterrent.

With these insights, we developed a data-driven strategy to enhance voter registration efforts. This local group refined its outreach approach, prioritizing short-form video content and leveraging peer-to-peer digital engagement rather than relying on mass email campaigns. This shift led to a measurable increase in voter registrations within the target demographic. While there is still progress to be made, this initiative underscores the power of

> generational data in shaping more effective engagement strategies and ensuring outreach efforts resonate with the intended audience.

Data can also be a powerful tool for fostering inclusivity. By monitoring generational diversity metrics at every level of the organization, companies can identify representation gaps and take steps to build a more equitable workplace. Even starting small, such as reviewing twelve months of retention data to spot patterns—like departments with higher turnover or entry-level roles with poor retention—can yield actionable insights. Taking these steps ensures organizations don't just react to workforce challenges but proactively build stronger, more resilient teams. This success story illustrates the power of workforce data when applied strategically.

So how can you begin collecting and using these valuable insights? Start with three proven approaches: pulse engagement surveys, 360-degree feedback, and employee journey mapping. Each of these tools offers a unique way to understand your team's needs, identify areas for improvement, and craft solutions that drive meaningful change.

> **PRO TIP:** Start small. Analyze your last twelve months of retention data. Look for patterns—departments with high turnover, entry-level roles that don't stick, or underutilized high-performers—and act.

2. Preparing for Future Generations

The workforce of tomorrow is evolving at an unprecedented pace. Generation Alpha, born between 2010 and 2024[12], and Generation Beta, born after 2025, will step into workplaces shaped by advances in AI, increasingly virtual and tech-integrated work environments, and the rapid acceleration of generational shifts. Their expectations will differ vastly from even the newer Gen Z members of the workforce today. Imagine employees who have never known a world without generative AI or the convenience of seamless digital automation. The question isn't whether change is coming—it's how we'll adapt to meet it.

Organizations that struggle to engage with Gen Z today risk being unprepared for what's next. Generational Performance Solutions' framework equips leaders with the tools to navigate these uncertainties, offering actionable insights to ensure teams remain agile, forward-thinking, and aligned with the future workforce.

To prepare for this next wave of talent, leaders must adopt a proactive mindset. Staying informed through continuous monitoring of societal and workforce trends is crucial. For example, if data suggests younger professionals increasingly value hybrid work environments, are your policies evolving to accommodate those preferences? Thinking ahead means recognizing the shifts happening now and acting on them before they become challenges; it does not mean that you are giving in as leaders.

Equally important is creating an environment where innovation is present. Organizations that encourage creativity, experimentation, and cross-functional collaboration are better positioned to adapt.

> **Case Study: The Power of Employee Innovation**
> One technology company we worked with exemplified this. Struggling with inefficiencies in product development and internal collaboration, they launched an internal Innovation Incubator to harness employee-driven solutions. The results? A 25 percent reduction in project turnaround time and a 15 percent improvement in cross-team collaboration, all thanks to employee-led initiatives. Beyond solving immediate challenges, this initiative gave employees a greater sense of ownership and pride—key drivers of engagement and long-term retention.

Training and development are also vital. As technology like VR, AR, and AI continues to reshape industries, organizations must invest in equipping their workforce with future-ready skills. Emphasizing adaptability, AI literacy, and digital tools ensures employees aren't just keeping up—they're leading.

Generational change is inevitable, but preparation is a choice. Reflecting on how past generations shaped workplaces can guide us forward. Baby boomers brought stability and structure. Gen X redefined leadership with self-reliance and adaptability, challenging rigid corporate hierarchies while advocating for work-life balance. Millennials ushered in flexibility and purpose-driven work. Gen Z is advocating for mental health resources and authenticity. With Generation Alpha on the horizon bringing entirely new expectations, the organizations that plan ahead will be the ones thriving amid disruption.

When organizations embrace data to inform decisions, the impact is transformative. High-performing teams feel valued, turnover decreases, and cultures become resilient to change. The future of the workforce isn't something to fear—it's an opportunity to lead. The time to prepare is now. Will your organization be ready?

KEY TAKEAWAYS FROM CHAPTER 10:

- Data is a competitive advantage. Organizations that use workforce data to guide decisions see improved retention, engagement, and innovation.
- Generational insights drive action. Understanding generational preferences isn't enough; companies must act on this knowledge to optimize recruitment and retention.
- Leaders who embrace continuous learning and evolving workforce expectations will build resilient, future-proof organizations.
- Workforce trends are shifting rapidly! Generations Alpha and Beta will reshape workplaces, requiring organizations to adopt forward-thinking strategies today.

 **Your Next Steps**

Here are practical steps to start leveraging data for today and tomorrow:

1. **Audit Your Current Data:** What are you already tracking (i.e., retention rates, engagement surveys), and are there any gaps in your insights?
2. **Build a Future-Ready Strategy:** Develop flexible scenario-based strategies to prepare for workforce changes and identify areas where AI or advanced training can future-proof your teams.
3. **Focus on Continuous Learning:** Launch programs that upskill employees to handle emerging technologies and future challenges.

4. **Engage Your Team:** Involve employees at all levels in discussions about innovation and future planning.

Data is both about looking back and looking forward. By combining insights about today's workforce with preparation for what's next, you can create a dynamic, resilient organization that inspires connection across generations and lives out the Generational Advantage.

> Dive deeper with your downloadable worksheet and apply what you've learned right away. Visit: https://thegenerationaladvantage.com/get-downloads/

Now, let's put it all together in Chapter 11 as we finalize the GPS Talent Impact Process.

CHAPTER 11

THE FORMULA: PUTTING THE PIECES TOGETHER

Throughout this book, we introduced you to the GPS Talent Impact Process, a proven strategic approach to help organizations cultivate dynamic multigenerational workplaces where every employee feels valued and motivated.

I don't have to tell you that building a thriving multigenerational team isn't easy. In fact, finding and keeping good talent feels harder than ever. Miscommunication, poor expectations, a lack of culture, and outdated strategies can leave leaders frustrated and teams fragmented.

But it doesn't have to be this way. The Talent Impact Process is here to help.

> Dive deeper with your downloadable worksheet and apply what you've learned right away. Visit: https://thegenerationaladvantage.com/get-downloads/

The Talent Impact Process: A Tool for Transformation

The Talent Impact Process is a dynamic system where every piece works together to:

- Enhance communication across all levels and generations.
- Attract, retain, and activate top talent for the long term.
- Develop culture and innovation that future-proofs your organization.
- Leverage data to make smarter decisions and prepare for tomorrow.

Let's review the steps, reconnect the pieces, and discuss how you can bring it all together.

1. Generational Excellence (The Foundation)
We started here for a reason: You must understand and value the strengths of each generation to build cohesion. Generational awareness sets the foundation for everything that follows.

Start with This:

- Launch an intergenerational training program to break down silos and encourage empathy. Our team is here as a resource if you're not sure where to begin.
- Facilitate conversations that identify similarities and strengths between generations without focusing solely on differences.

THE FORMULA: PUTTING THE PIECES TOGETHER

Why It Matters: Without generational awareness, friction remains unaddressed and collaboration falters.

2. Attraction (Culture First, Services Second)
Attracting top talent today requires authenticity, strategy, and a clear understanding of where candidates live online and offline.

How to Get Started:

- Conduct an audit of your digital presence: website, social media, and hiring tools (think: job descriptions, job ads). Is your brand reflective of your culture and values?
- Highlight employee success stories and internal culture wins—your future hires are watching.

Why It Matters: Companies that attract talent based on culture—not just compensation—build stronger, more loyal teams.

3. Onboarding and Development (Set the Trajectory Early)
Onboarding is much more than the first week of work, which you should hopefully know by now. It's critical to laying the groundwork for an employee's entire career. When done right, it fuels retention, growth, and satisfaction.

How to Get Started:

- Extend your onboarding process beyond two to three weeks—create a ninety-day framework that clarifies expectations, milestones, and growth pathways.
- Launch mentorship programs, including two-way mentoring, to integrate younger and more experienced employees.

Why It Matters: A great onboarding experience ensures employees feel supported from day one, reducing turnover and increasing engagement.

4. Retention and Activation (Beyond Retaining Talent—Activate Potential)
Keeping talent is only half the goal. Activating employees to realize their full potential is what drives culture and performance.

Don't Just Retain—Activate By:

- Offering continuous professional development that's customized to employee strengths and goals.
- Engaging employees in decision-making processes, ensuring all voices (not solely leadership) are heard.

Why It Matters: Activation boosts engagement, loyalty, and productivity—turning your employees into champions of your business.

5. Communication and Expectations (The Activator)
Communication—when done well—connects all the dots. Without it, your teams are working hard, but not together.

Set Clear Expectations By:

- Mapping out communication guidelines: when to email, when to Slack, and how to escalate urgent issues.
- Regularly asking your teams "How do you like to be communicated with?" and acknowledging those preferences.

Why It Matters: Misaligned communication is the number one culprit of team breakdowns. Clarity creates alignment and trust.

6. Culture (The Glue That Holds It All Together)
Culture isn't one initiative or one team event—it's the lived experience of every employee, shaped by values, behaviors, and beliefs.

Consider This:

- Do your core values guide daily behaviors, decision-making, and leadership actions? If not, revisit and reinforce them.
- Promote inclusion by ensuring all generations have a seat at the table, not just in token roles, but in leadership and planning conversations.

Why It Matters: A strong culture is the single most powerful driver of retention, productivity, and satisfaction.

7. Data (Your Compass for Today—and Tomorrow)
You can't improve what you don't measure. Data helps you understand your workforce today while preparing for the challenges and opportunities of tomorrow.

How to Start Leveraging Data:

- Analyze retention trends, engagement surveys, and recruitment success to identify patterns and gaps.
- Develop strategies for future generations (like Gen Alpha) by monitoring trends in technology, communication preferences, and workplace expectations.

Why It Matters: Data provides a clear picture of where your organization stands today and helps you make informed decisions that shape its future.

How It All Connects

Once you put the Talent Impact Process into practice, you will see that all its pieces work together like gears in a well-oiled machine. If one part is neglected, the system fails. Don't let your system be the one to do it. Remember that when working in tandem, you will find that:

- Generational Excellence ensures mutual understanding.
- Attraction brings in the right people.
- Onboarding and Development sets them up for success.
- Retention and Activation deepens their connection and growth.
- Communication and Expectations activates alignment.
- Culture reinforces purpose and belonging.
- Data ensures you can measure progress and look to the future.

Together, these steps form a sustainable strategy for building a multigenerational workforce where everyone thrives. The results will speak for themselves.

Final Thoughts: Your Multigenerational Legacy Starts Here

Generational change will continue happening—faster than ever. AI, remote work, and new workplace norms will challenge the way we hire, lead, and communicate. But leaders who adopt the Talent Impact Process won't be adapting; they will prosper.

At GPS, we believe the future of work belongs to companies that:

- See generational diversity as a strength, not a challenge.
- Proactively prepare for the workforce of tomorrow.
- Invest in their employees at every stage of their careers.

THE FORMULA: PUTTING THE PIECES TOGETHER

The Talent Impact Process isn't a quick fix. It's a journey—one that requires intention, effort, and time. But if you've made it this far, you're already on the path to creating a workforce where every employee feels valued, respected, and activated.

 Your Next Steps

1. **Revisit the Wheel:** Assess where your organization shines and where you need to focus. For a personalized assessment and to see how your organization stacks up across all areas of the Talent Impact Process, visit www.genperformance.com.
2. **Create Your Action Plan:** Start small. Pick one step of the Talent Impact Process to implement over the next ninety days.
3. **Measure, Adjust, and Grow:** Use data to track progress, refine your approach, and celebrate wins.
4. **Reread This Book:** Come back to this resource as much as you need to cross-reference your plans, retrace your steps, and use it as your playbook for your thriving multigenerational workforce.

The future of the workforce—and your organization's legacy—starts now.

Ready to transform your workplace? Let's do it together.

CHAPTER 12

THE FUTURE OF WORK: THRIVING IN THE AI-DRIVEN, MULTIGENERATIONAL ERA

The workforce is evolving faster than ever. Artificial intelligence is transforming how we work, automation is redefining job roles, and new generations are entering the workplace with vastly different expectations. As leaders, we are not just managing today's workforce—we are shaping the future.

Throughout this book, we have explored the GPS Talent Impact Process, a framework designed to create a multigenerational workforce where employees feel valued, engaged, and motivated. The Talent Impact Process helps organizations build workplaces that work for everyone, across all generations, ensuring companies remain adaptable, competitive, and innovative. But the journey does not end here.

The final piece of the puzzle is the future. While we have examined how to attract, retain, develop, and activate today's workforce, we must also look ahead to how work itself is changing. Leaders who embrace the Generational Advantage—who understand that leveraging generational diversity is a competitive edge—will be the ones who prosper in this new era. Those who resist change, who cling to outdated models of leadership and talent management, will find themselves struggling to keep up.

The question is no longer *if* the workplace will change, but *how prepared your organization will be* when it does.

The AI Revolution and the Multigenerational Workforce

Artificial intelligence is no longer a concept of the future; it is here, embedded in everything from recruiting software to workflow automation. Companies have already been using AI to streamline hiring, analyze employee engagement, and predict workforce trends. As technology continues to evolve, leaders must recognize that AI is not replacing people—it is redefining their roles.

This shift means that traditional methods of hiring, training, and leading teams are quickly becoming obsolete. Skills-based hiring is overtaking degree-based hiring as companies prioritize real-world capabilities over formal credentials. Routine administrative tasks are being automated, freeing employees to focus on more strategic and creative work. The ability to adapt to these changes will define an organization's success, but you likely already know that.

At the same time, generational shifts are accelerating. Generation Alpha (born 2010–2024) will enter the workforce within the next decade, bringing expectations that are shaped by a fully digital upbringing, AI-integrated learning, and a workplace culture unlike anything seen before. Leaders who struggled to engage Gen Z will need to rethink their entire approach when managing a generation (we're talking about Generation Alpha now) that has never known a world without automation and instant access to data.

The Generational Advantage remains crucial in this transformation. AI can provide data-driven insights, but it cannot replace the human aspects of leadership—mentorship, collaboration, innovation, and emotional intelligence. The most successful companies will be those that merge technology with multigenerational expertise, ensuring that experience and innovation work together, rather than in competition.

What Happens If You Don't (Leverage This Information)?

One of my favorite ways to end a keynote is by telling my audience they don't have to follow my advice. But—what happens if they don't? So I'm asking you the same question. Failing to embrace these changes does not mean your organization will remain the same—it means your organization will fall behind. Are you willing to take that risk?

Here's what happens when leaders ignore the Generational Advantage and the trends shaping the future of work, based on our work with more than two thousand organizations across North America:

- Talent Drain and High Turnover: Companies that do not adapt to workforce expectations will struggle to attract and retain top talent. Younger generations will seek out employers who prioritize flexibility, inclusion, and purpose-driven work.
- Culture Breakdown: Ignoring generational diversity creates disengagement, miscommunication, and a toxic culture where employees feel unheard or undervalued.
- Loss of Competitive Edge: Companies that resist AI and workforce data analytics will lack the insights necessary to make informed hiring, engagement, and retention decisions.
- Inefficiency and Declining Productivity: Organizations that fail to embrace AI and automation will waste time on outdated processes, while competitors gain efficiency through innovation.
- Irrelevance in the Marketplace: The workforce is evolving. Companies that refuse to evolve with it will struggle to remain relevant, losing out to more agile, forward-thinking competitors.

The choice is clear: Adapt and thrive or resist and struggle.

The Future of Work Is Hybrid, Flexible, and Global

Even before AI's rapid expansion, workplace trends were shifting. The rise of hybrid work, flexible job models, and global talent pools has changed how organizations think about workforce management. Employees are no longer limited by location, and companies that once relied on in-person collaboration must now embrace digital-first environments.

The Talent Impact Process remains as relevant as ever in this shift. Without intentional communication and strong culture-building, hybrid teams risk becoming disconnected. Without clear expectations and structured onboarding, new hires will struggle to engage with their teams. And without data-driven decision-making, companies will miss critical trends that could determine their ability to attract and retain top talent.

Organizations that fail to adapt to these realities will not only lose out on talent but will struggle to remain competitive. The new workforce is mobile, deeply connected to purpose-driven work, and spans across multiple generations. Employers who embrace flexibility—who prioritize outcomes over outdated workplace norms—will have access to the best and brightest talent, regardless of where they are located.

Future-Proofing Leadership in the AI Era

While technology and workplace structures are evolving, leadership must evolve even faster. The leaders who will thrive in the coming decades will be those who embrace continuous learning, digital fluency, and cross-generational collaboration.

The essential leadership traits of the AI era revolve around adaptability, digital fluency, and human-centered leadership. Leaders must be able to pivot strategies in response to evolving technology and workforce trends while developing a foundational understanding of AI and data analytics to make informed decisions. However, technical expertise alone is not enough—emotional intelligence, empathy, and inclusion remain critical, as AI cannot replace human connection. Building a culture rooted in trust, collaboration, and psychological safety keeps employees engaged and motivated. Additionally, effective leaders must embrace cross-generational leadership, recognizing and leveraging the strengths of each generation so that experience and innovation work together rather than in isolation.

Final Call to Action: Building a Future-Ready Workforce

The future of work is not just about technology—it is about people. The Talent Impact Process has given you the tools to create a thriving, multigenerational workforce today, but the most successful organizations will be those that use it to prepare for tomorrow.

The workforce will continue to evolve at an unprecedented pace. The companies that embrace AI, generational diversity, and workplace flexibility will not only survive—they will lead the future of work.

If you're reading this book years from now, the specifics of the workplace may have changed, but the need for strong, adaptable leadership has not. The GPS Talent Impact Process is designed to evolve with time—use it as a guide to navigate whatever the workforce looks like today.

The Generational Advantage is so much more than understanding differences—it is about seeing generational diversity as a business asset. Companies that apply the Talent Impact Process alongside emerging workplace trends will be the ones that attract, retain, and activate the best talent for years to come.

Your Next Steps

1. **Assess Your Readiness:** How can your organization adopt AI, support hybrid work, and engage future generations?
2. **Develop a Future-Proof Talent Strategy:** Start integrating skills-based hiring, digital-first leadership training, and cross-generational mentorship into your long-term workforce plan.
3. **Invest in Continuous Learning:** Ensure that your leadership and employees are prepared for the evolving landscape through ongoing development.
4. **Lead with Purpose and Adaptability:** Organizations that commit to innovation, flexibility, and Generational Excellence will be the ones that shape the future of work.

The question is no longer whether the workplace will evolve. *It already has.* The real challenge is deciding what role you will play in its future. Will you wait for change to dictate your path, or will you harness *the Generational Advantage* to lead the way forward? The choice is yours.

ACKNOWLEDGEMENTS

The Generational Advantage would not be possible without the support of so many people.

First, I'd like to thank my dad for encouraging me—years ago—to write this book. My family, including my mom and brother, have supported me from the very beginning, but my dad has always seen the value in this project as a way to elevate the work I do. His nudges were the spark that got me here.

To my husband, Clay—thank you for being my rock through it all. You've witnessed me writing at odd hours, across time zones, and between meetings over the last two years. You've been my greatest support system.

To my GPS team: thank you for reviewing, listening, contributing, and believing in the work we do. Jade, Christine, Barkley—your dedication to the business means more than you'll ever know.

To the reviewers and partners who helped shape and refine this book—thank you. Your thoughtful feedback, edits, and encouragement elevated the final product. Whether you reviewed a single chapter or the full manuscript, your insight made a difference, and I am deeply grateful.

To the original YoPro Know supporters—our first clients, advisors, and blog interviewees—thank you. Your willingness to share your stories helped build what is now Generational Performance Solutions.

To my mentors—both long-standing and new—thank you for guiding me through this entrepreneurial journey, especially during the most intense phases of writing, editing, and publishing. You know who you are, and I am endlessly grateful.

And finally, to everyone who has followed along on this journey to better understand generations in the workplace: Thank you. Over the past decade, generational content has surged in popularity. My hope is that, through this work—and the work of so many others—we can build something that lasts. Not a trend, but a true movement.

SOURCES

1. Dimock, Michael. "Defining generations: Where Millennials end and Generation Z begins." *Pew Research Center* (*Short Reads*), January 17, 2019. https://www.pewresearch.org/short-reads/2019/01/17/where-millennials-end-and-generation-z-begins/.
2. "U.S. Fertility Rate Drops to Another Historic Low," *National Center for Health Statistics, CDC*. Last reviewed April 25, 2024. https://www.cdc.gov/nchs/pressroom/nchs_press_releases/2024/20240525.htm.
3. Perna, Mark C. "Why Gen Z Is Thriving in the Entrepreneurial Life." *Forbes*, June 18, 2024. https://www.forbes.com/sites/markcperna/2024/06/18/gen-z-thriving-entrepreneurship/.
4. Tatel, Corey, and Ben Wigert. "42% of Employee Turnover Is Preventable but Often Ignored." *Gallup*, July 10, 2024. https://www.gallup.com/workplace/646538/employee-turnover-preventable-often-ignored.aspx.
5. Chouinard, Yvon. *Let My People Go Surfing: The Education of a Reluctant Businessman*. New York: Penguin Books, 2016.
6. Gallup. "A Fixable Problem That Costs Businesses a Trillion." https://www.gallup.com/workplace/247391/fixable-problem-costs-businesses-trillion.aspx.
7. Pendell, Ryan, and Sara Vander Helm. "Generation Disconnected: Data of Gen Z in the Workplace." *Gallup*, November 11, 2022. https://www.gallup.com/workplace/404693/generation-disconnected-data-gen-workplace.aspx.

8   Royle, Orianna Rosa. "1 in 5 Gen Zers Haven't Had a Single Conversation with Someone over 50 in Their Workplace in the Last Year, LinkedIn Research Says." *Fortune*, December 11, 2024. https://fortune.com/article/gen-z-boomers-gen-x-linkedin-workplace-afraid-salary-talk/.

9   Haidt, Jonathan. *The Anxious Generation: How the Great Rewiring of Childhood Is Causing an Epidemic of Mental Illness.* New York: Penguin, 2024. https://www.anxiousgeneration.com/book.

10 "Demographics of Social Media." *Pew Research*, November 13, 2024. https://www.pewresearch.org/internet/fact-sheet/social-media/.

11 Fisher, Jen, Sue Cantrell, Jay Bhatt, and Paul H. Silverglate. "The Important Role of Leaders in Advancing Human Sustainability." *Deloitte*, June 18, 2024. https://www2.deloitte.com/us/en/insights/topics/talent/workplace-well-being-research-2024.html.

12 "Understanding Generation Alpha." *McCrindle*. https://mccrindle.com.au/article/topic/generation-alpha/generation-alpha-defined/.